The Rise of Sorceress Issues 1-4

Written, Illustrated, Inked, and Colored by Jessica Johnson

D1530118

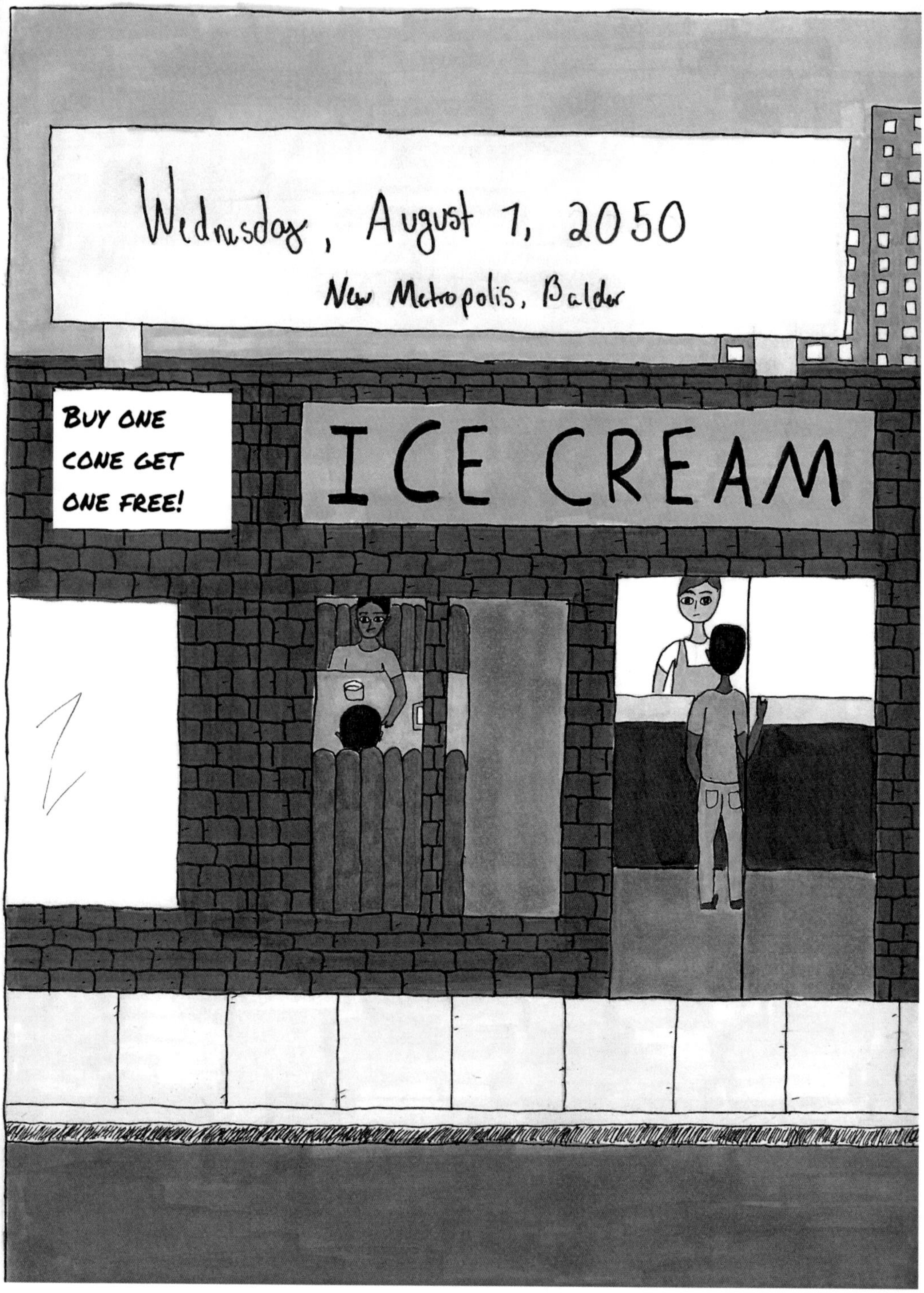
Wednesday, August 1, 2050
New Metropolis, Balder
BUY ONE CONE GET ONE FREE!
ICE CREAM

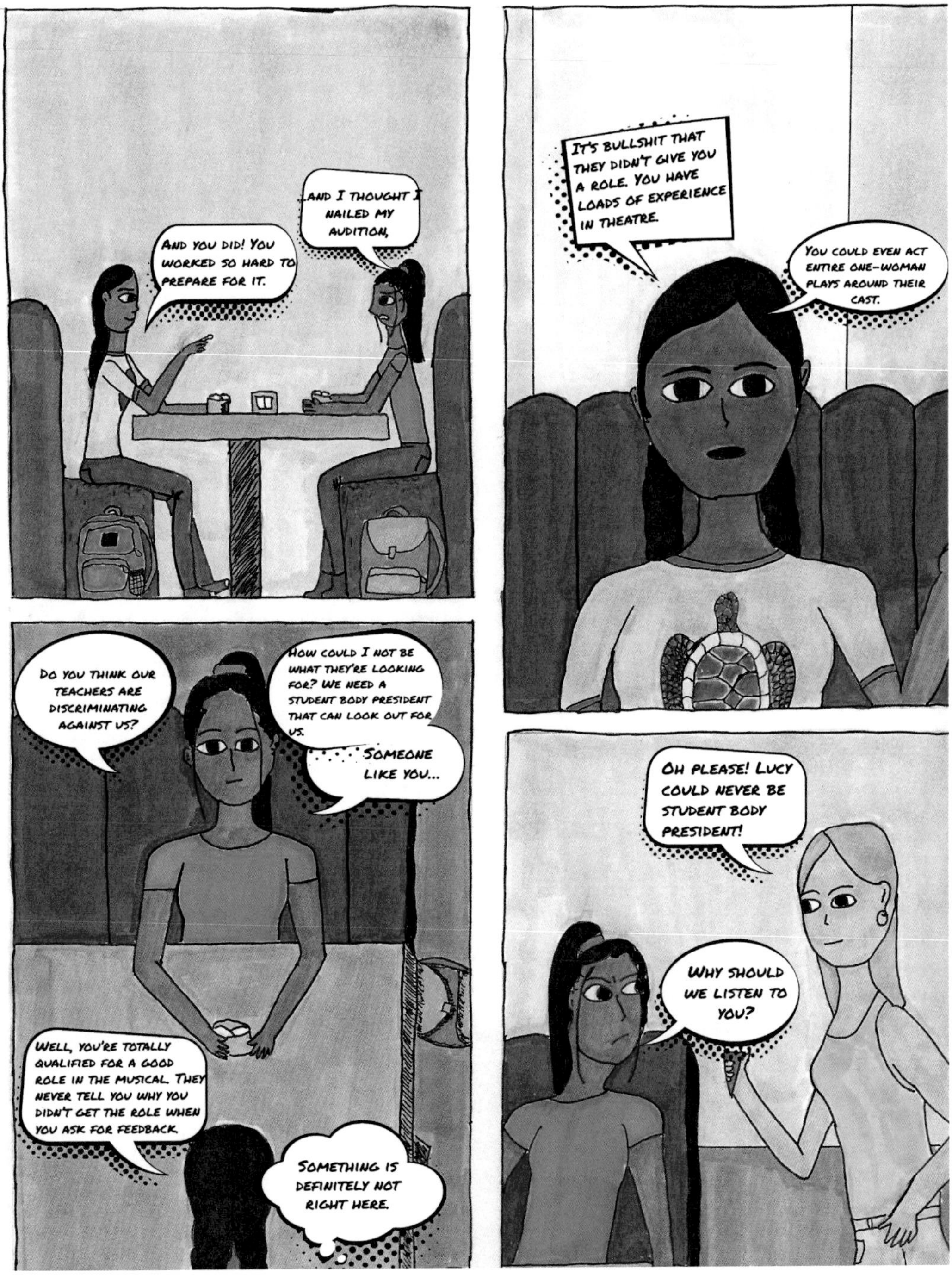
...and I thought I nailed my audition,
And you did! You worked so hard to prepare for it.
It's bullshit that they didn't give you a role. You have loads of experience in theatre.
You could even act entire one-woman plays around their cast.
Do you think our teachers are discriminating against us?
How could I not be what they're looking for? We need a student body president that can look out for us.
Someone like you...
Well, you're totally qualified for a good role in the musical. They never tell you why you didn't get the role when you ask for feedback.
Something is definitely not right here.
Oh please! Lucy could never be student body president!
Why should we listen to you?

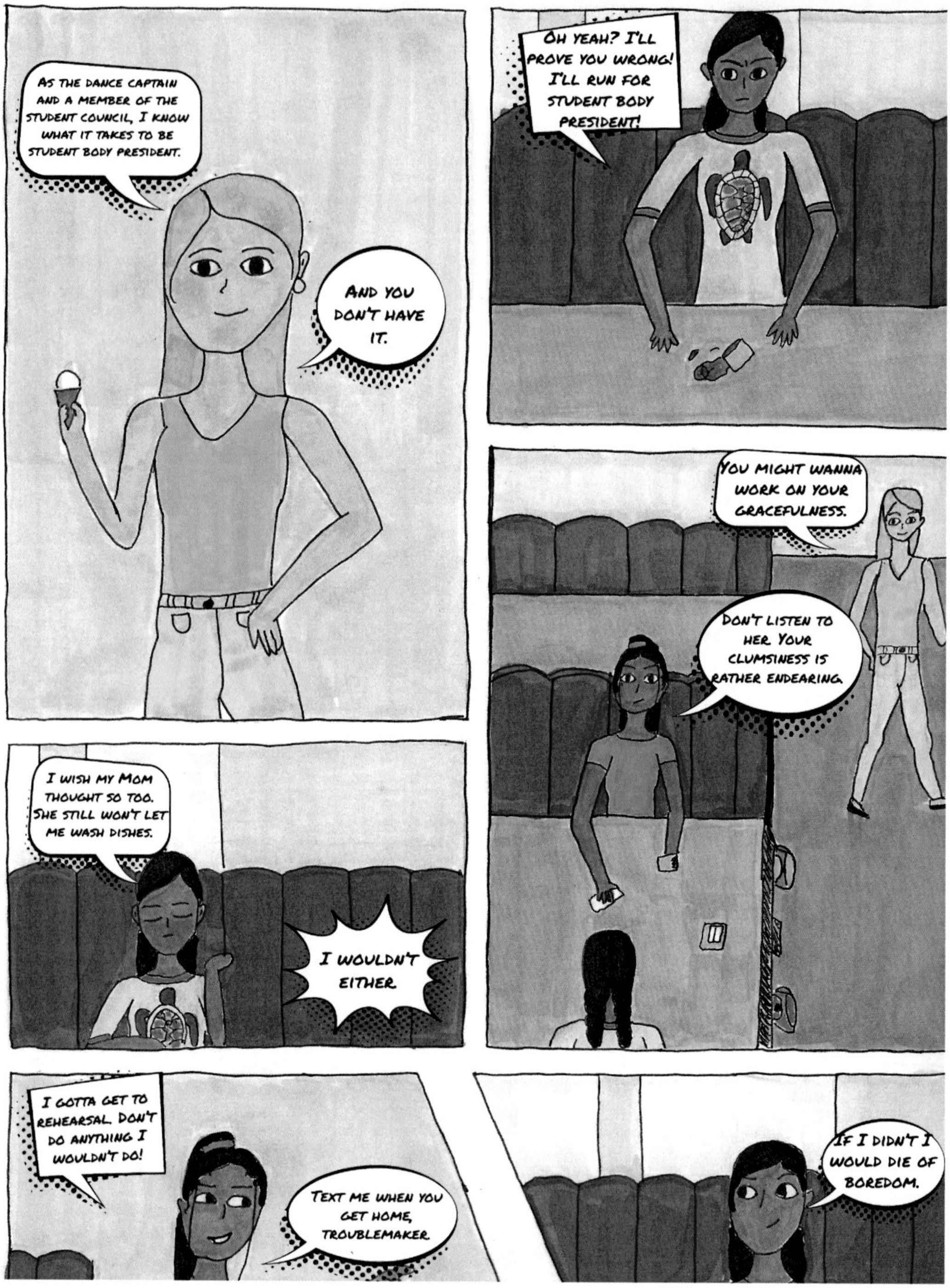
As the dance captain and a member of the student council, I know what it takes to be student body president.
And you don't have it.
Oh yeah? I'll prove you wrong! I'll run for student body president!
You might wanna work on your gracefulness.
Don't listen to her. Your clumsiness is rather endearing.
I wish my Mom thought so too. She still won't let me wash dishes.
I wouldn't either.
I gotta get to rehearsal. Don't do anything I wouldn't do!
Text me when you get home, troublemaker.
If I didn't I would die of boredom.

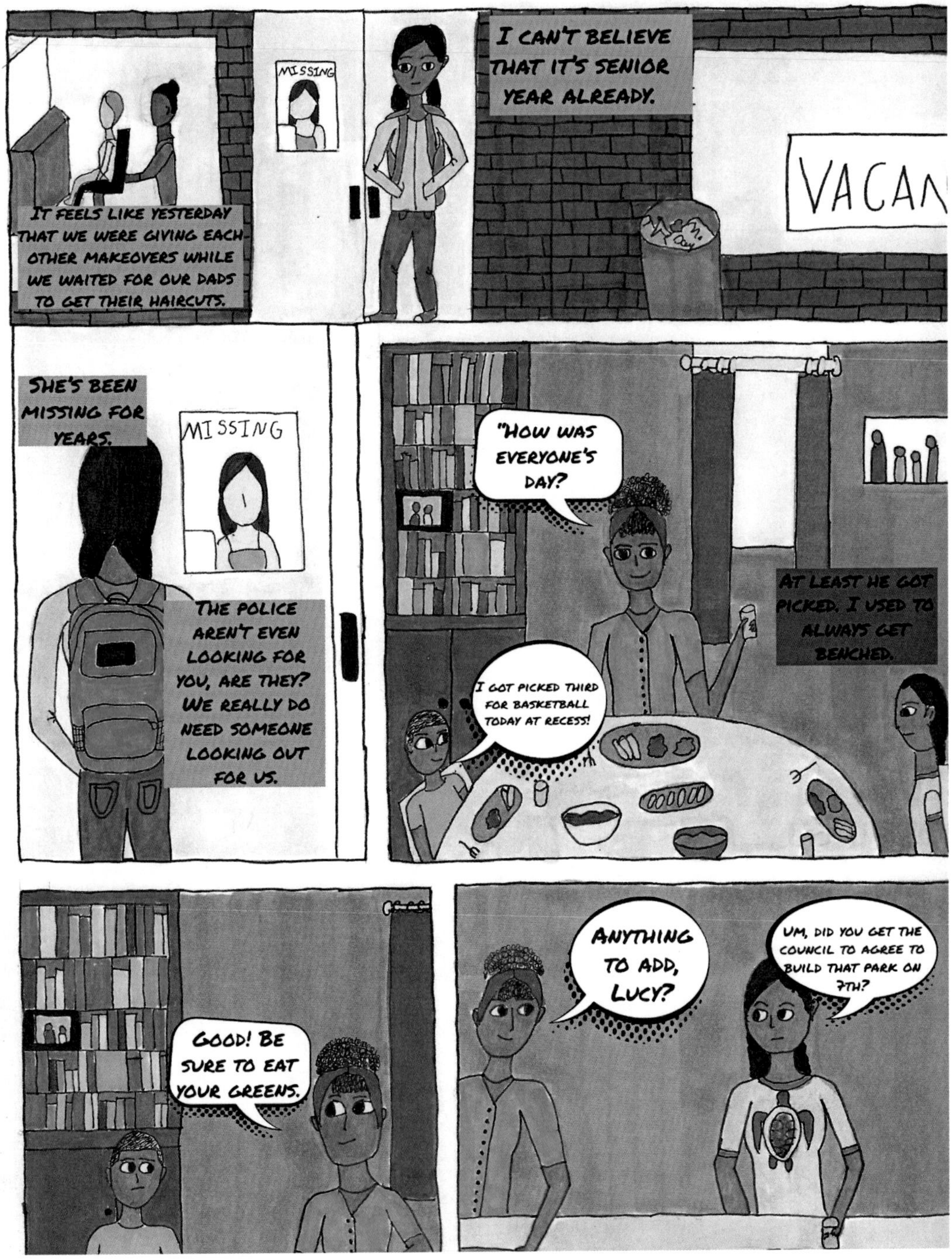
It feels like yesterday that we were giving each other makeovers while we waited for our dads to get their haircuts.
MISSING
I can't believe that it's senior year already.
VACAN
She's been missing for years.
MISSING
The police aren't even looking for you, are they? We really do need someone looking out for us.
"How was everyone's day?
At least he got picked. I used to always get benched.
I got picked third for basketball today at recess!
Good! Be sure to eat your greens.
Anything to add, Lucy?
Um, did you get the council to agree to build that park on 7th?

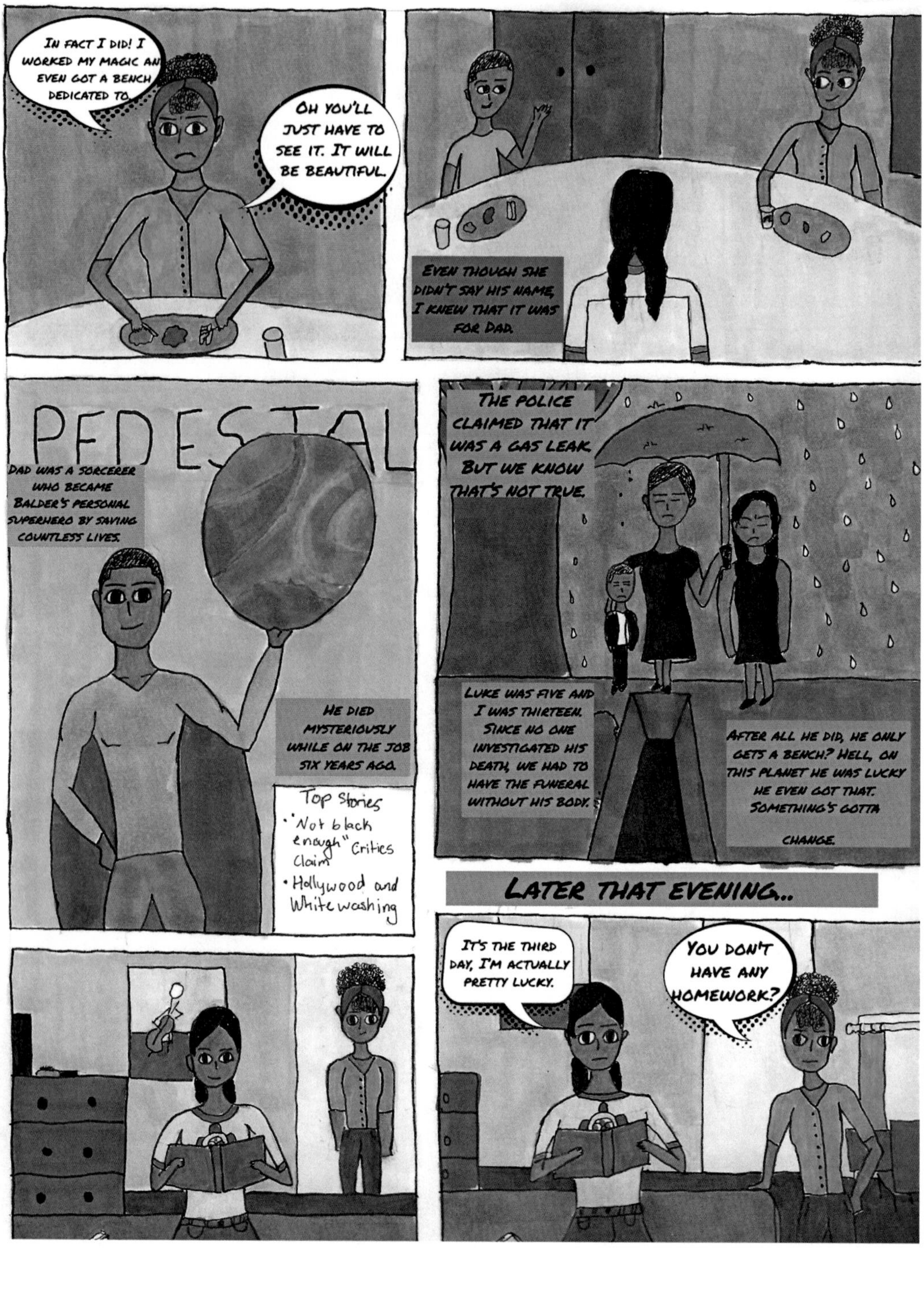
In fact I did! I worked my magic an even got a bench dedicated to.
Oh you'll just have to see it. It will be beautiful.
Even though she didn't say his name, I knew that it was for Dad.
PEDESTAL
Dad was a sorcerer who became Balder's personal superhero by saving countless lives.
He died mysteriously while on the job six years ago.
Top Stories
• "Not black enough" Critics Claim
• Hollywood and Whitewashing
The police claimed that it was a gas leak. But we know that's not true.
Luke was five and I was thirteen. Since no one investigated his death, we had to have the funeral without his body.
After all he did, he only gets a bench? Hell, on this planet he was lucky he even got that. Something's gotta change.
Later that evening..
You don't have any homework?
It's the third day, I'm actually pretty lucky.

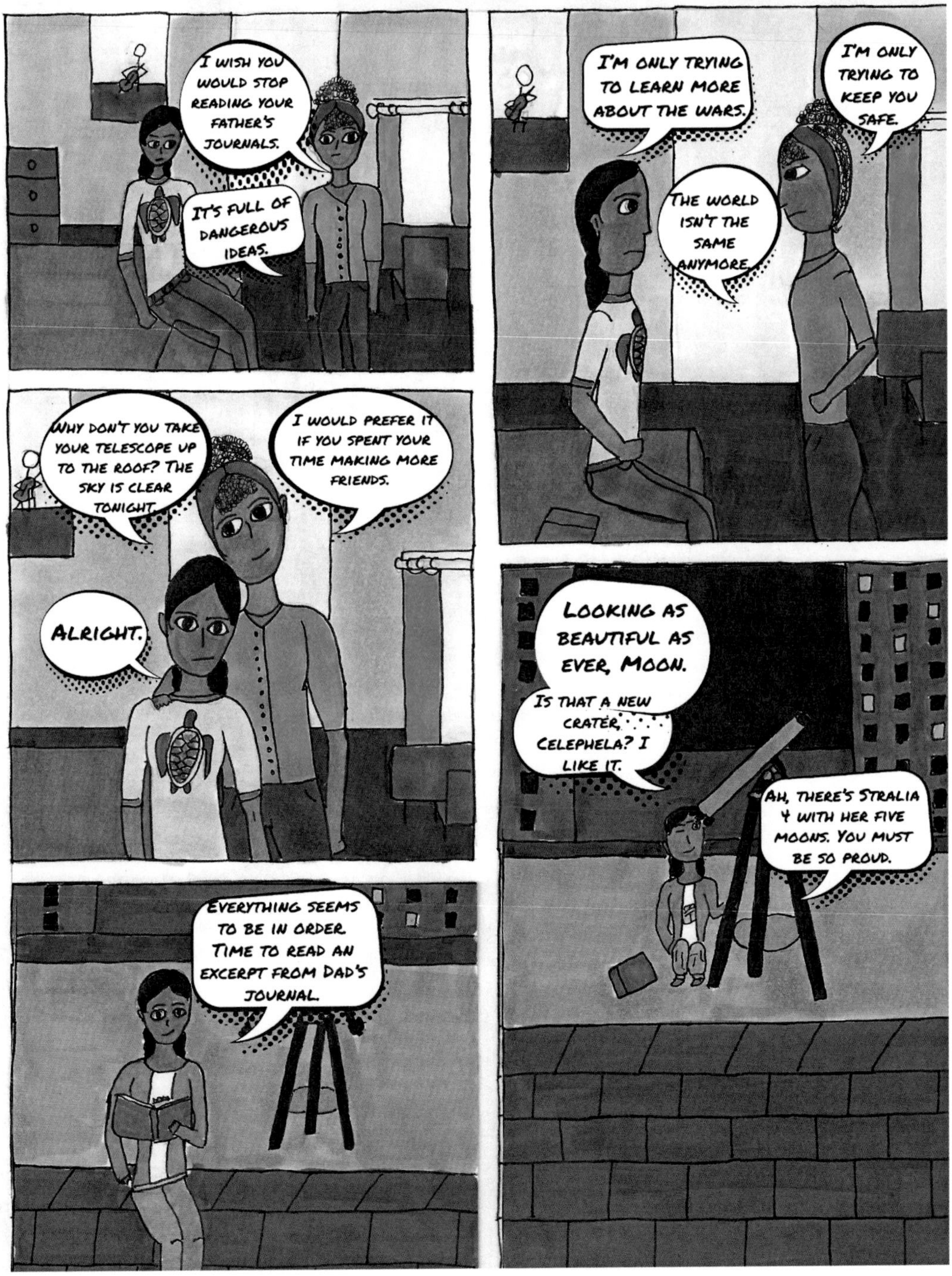
I wish you would stop reading your father's journals.
It's full of dangerous ideas.
I'm only trying to learn more about the wars.
I'm only trying to keep you safe.
The world isn't the same anymore.
Why don't you take your telescope up to the roof? The sky is clear tonight.
I would prefer it if you spent your time making more friends.
Alright.
Looking as beautiful as ever, Moon.
Is that a new crater, Celephela? I like it.
Ah, there's Stralia 4 with her five moons. You must be so proud.
Everything seems to be in order. Time to read an excerpt from Dad's journal.

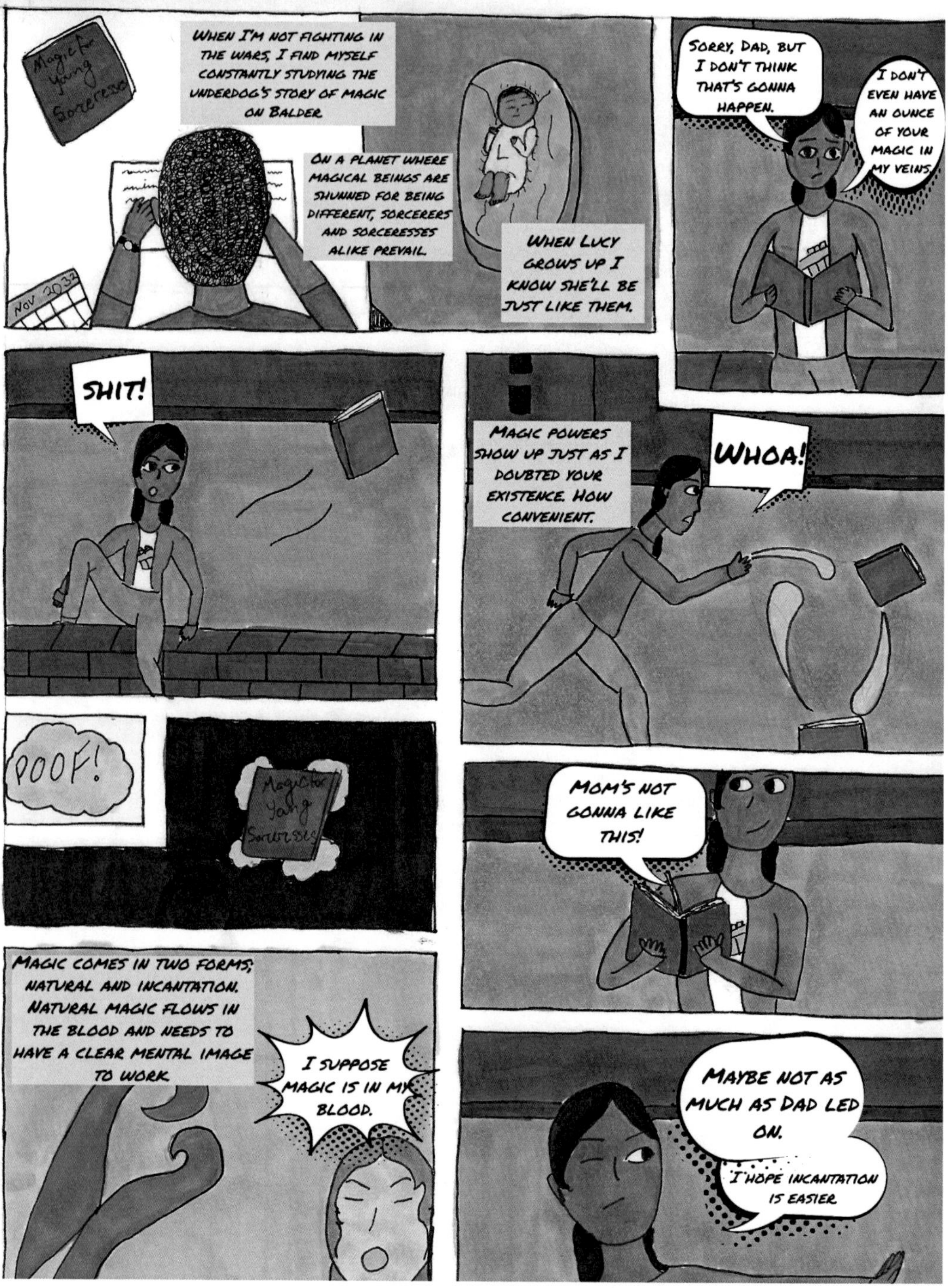

Magic for Young Sorceresses
When I'm not fighting in the wars, I find myself constantly studying the underdog's story of magic on Balder.
On a planet where magical beings are shunned for being different, sorcerers and sorceresses alike prevail.
Nov 2032
When Lucy grows up I know she'll be just like them.
Sorry, Dad, but I don't think that's gonna happen.
I don't even have an ounce of your magic in my veins.
SHIT!
Magic powers show up just as I doubted your existence. How convenient.
WHOA!
POOF!
Magic for Young Sorceresses
Mom's not gonna like this!
Magic comes in two forms; natural and incantation. Natural magic flows in the blood and needs to have a clear mental image to work.
I suppose magic is in my blood.
Maybe not as much as Dad led on.
I hope incantation is easier

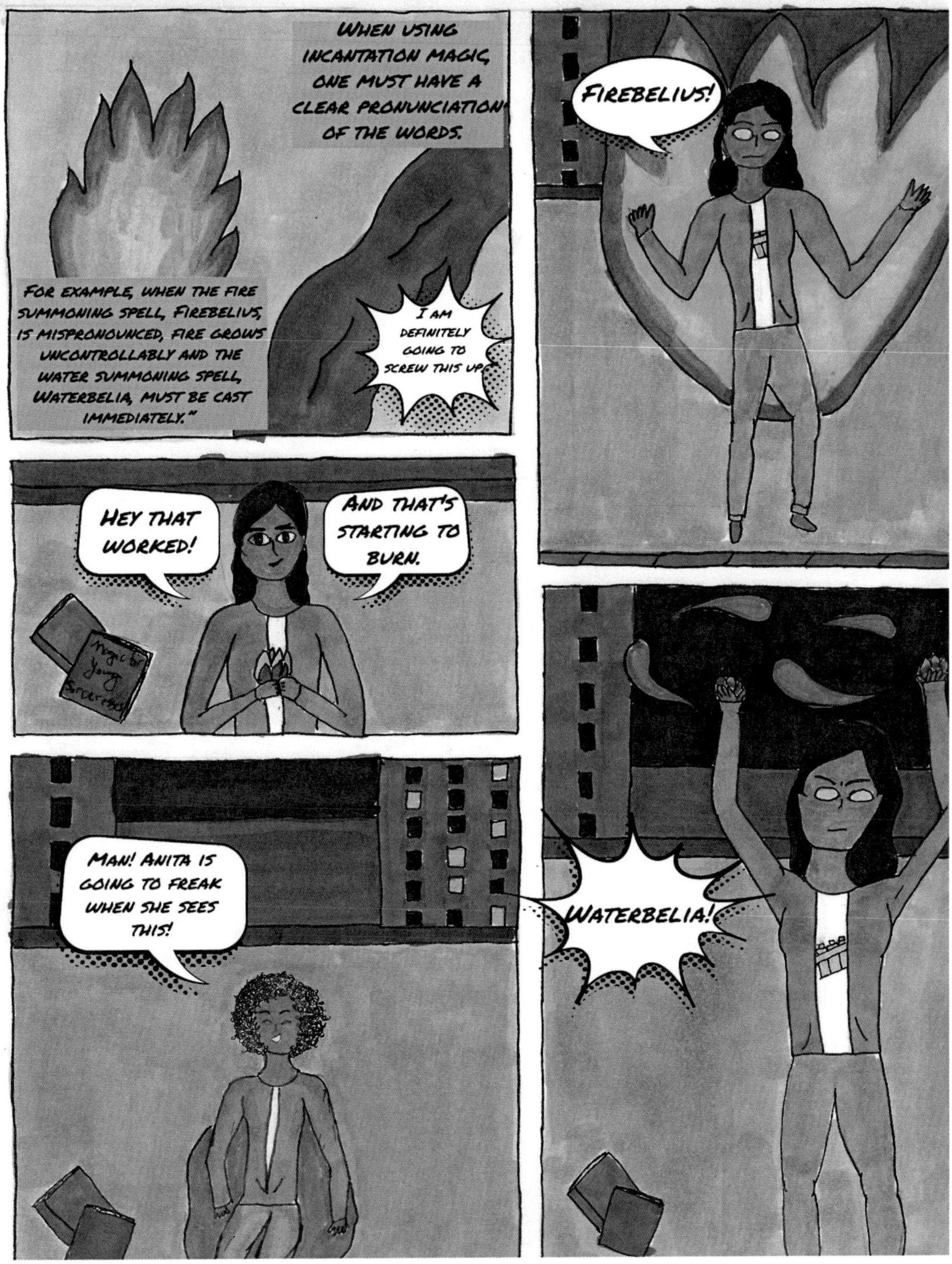
When using incantation magic, one must have a clear pronunciation of the words.
For example, when the fire summoning spell, Firebelius, is mispronounced, fire grows uncontrollably and the water summoning spell, Waterbelia, must be cast immediately."
I am definitely going to screw this up.
Firebelius!
Hey that worked!
And that's starting to burn.
Magic for Young Sorceresses
Waterbelia!
Man! Anita is going to freak when she sees this!

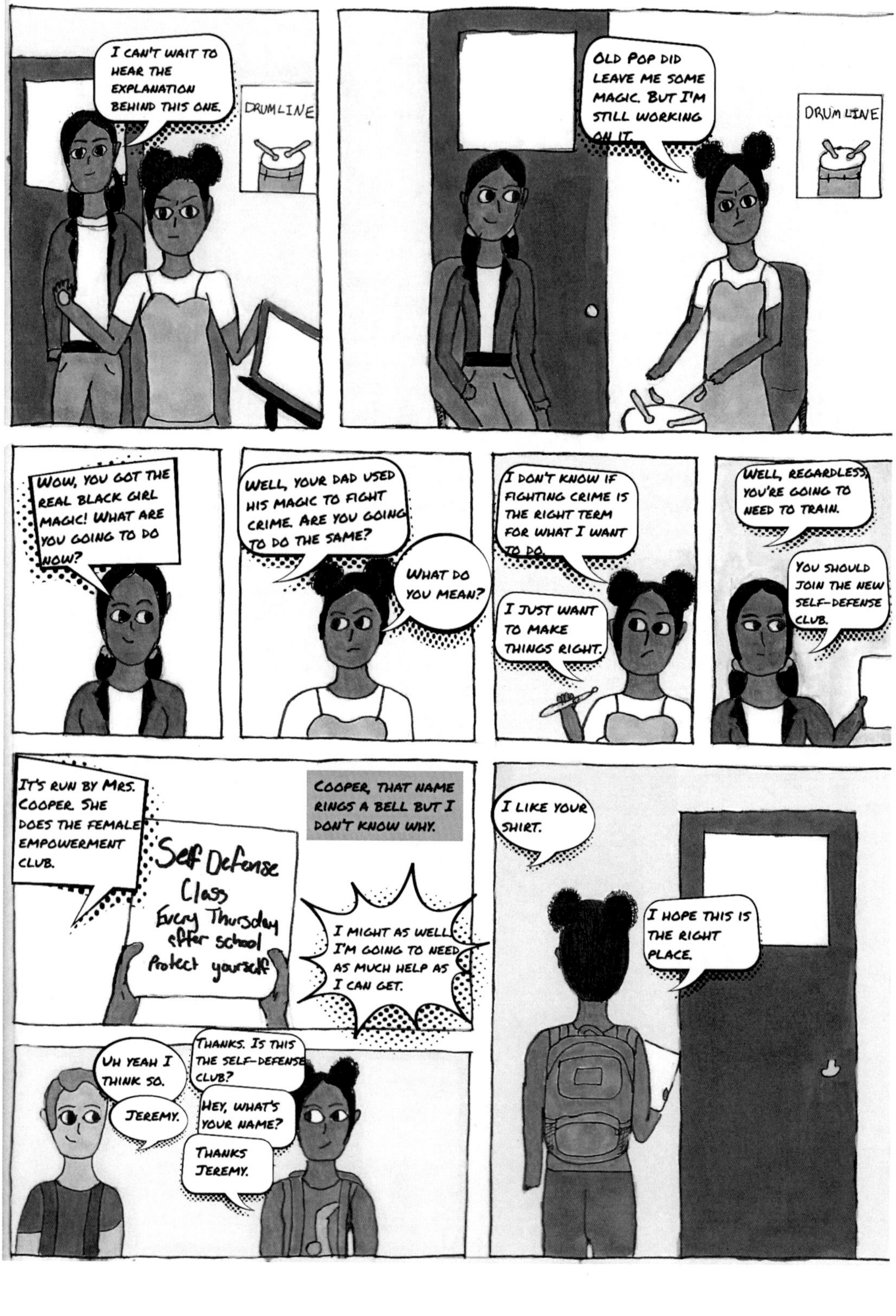
I CAN'T WAIT TO HEAR THE EXPLANATION BEHIND THIS ONE.
DRUMLINE
OLD POP DID LEAVE ME SOME MAGIC. BUT I'M STILL WORKING ON IT.
DRUMLINE
WOW, YOU GOT THE REAL BLACK GIRL MAGIC! WHAT ARE YOU GOING TO DO NOW?
WELL, YOUR DAD USED HIS MAGIC TO FIGHT CRIME. ARE YOU GOING TO DO THE SAME?
WHAT DO YOU MEAN?
I DON'T KNOW IF FIGHTING CRIME IS THE RIGHT TERM FOR WHAT I WANT TO DO.
I JUST WANT TO MAKE THINGS RIGHT.
WELL, REGARDLESS, YOU'RE GOING TO NEED TO TRAIN.
YOU SHOULD JOIN THE NEW SELF-DEFENSE CLUB.
IT'S RUN BY MRS. COOPER. SHE DOES THE FEMALE EMPOWERMENT CLUB.
Self Defense Class Every Thursday after school Protect yourself
COOPER, THAT NAME RINGS A BELL BUT I DON'T KNOW WHY.
I MIGHT AS WELL. I'M GOING TO NEED AS MUCH HELP AS I CAN GET.
I LIKE YOUR SHIRT.
I HOPE THIS IS THE RIGHT PLACE.
THANKS. IS THIS THE SELF-DEFENSE CLUB?
UH YEAH I THINK SO.
HEY, WHAT'S YOUR NAME?
JEREMY.
THANKS JEREMY.

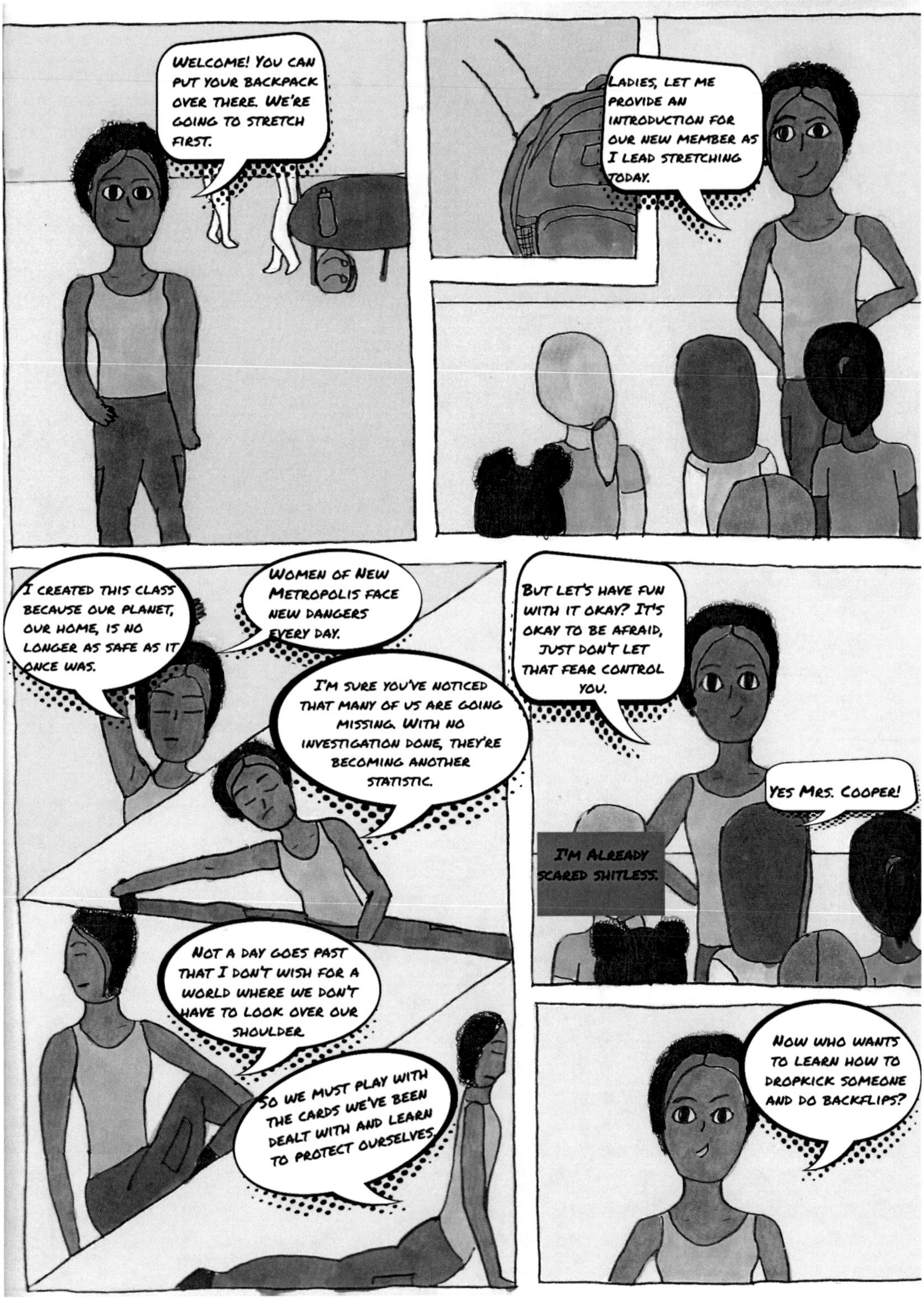

Welcome! You can put your backpack over there. We're going to stretch first.
Ladies, let me provide an introduction for our new member as I lead stretching today.
I created this class because our planet, our home, is no longer as safe as it once was.
Women of New Metropolis face new dangers every day.
I'm sure you've noticed that many of us are going missing. With no investigation done, they're becoming another statistic.
Not a day goes past that I don't wish for a world where we don't have to look over our shoulder.
So we must play with the cards we've been dealt with and learn to protect ourselves.
But let's have fun with it okay? It's okay to be afraid, just don't let that fear control you.
I'm already scared shitless.
Yes Mrs. Cooper!
Now who wants to learn how to dropkick someone and do backflips?

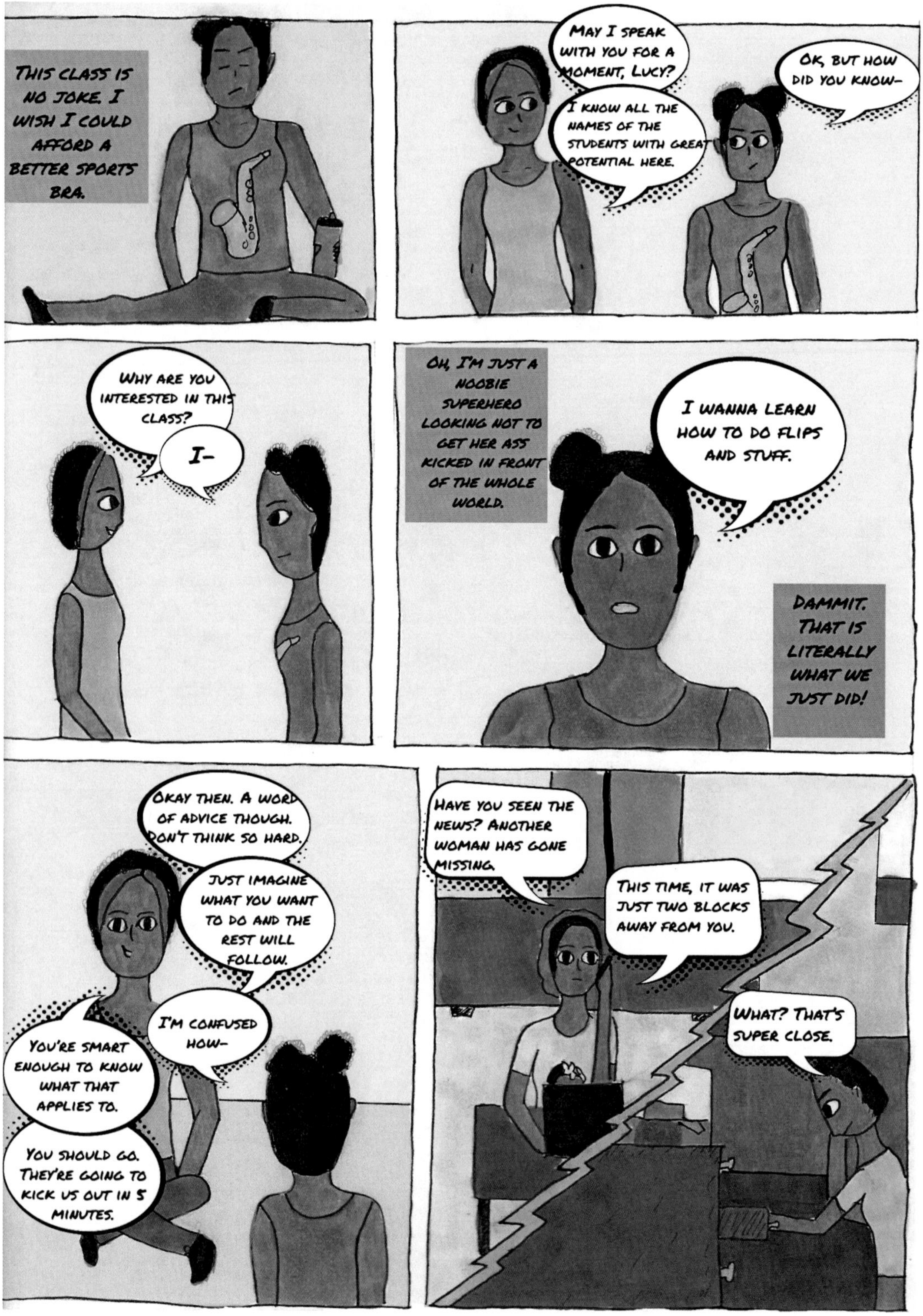
This class is no joke. I wish I could afford a better sports bra.
May I speak with you for a moment, Lucy?
I know all the names of the students with great potential here.
Ok, but how did you know-
Why are you interested in this class?
I-
Oh, I'm just a noobie superhero looking not to get her ass kicked in front of the whole world.
I wanna learn how to do flips and stuff.
Dammit. That is literally what we just did!
Okay then. A word of advice though. Don't think so hard.
Just imagine what you want to do and the rest will follow.
I'm confused how-
You're smart enough to know what that applies to.
You should go. They're going to kick us out in 5 minutes.
Have you seen the news? Another woman has gone missing.
This time, it was just two blocks away from you.
What? That's super close.

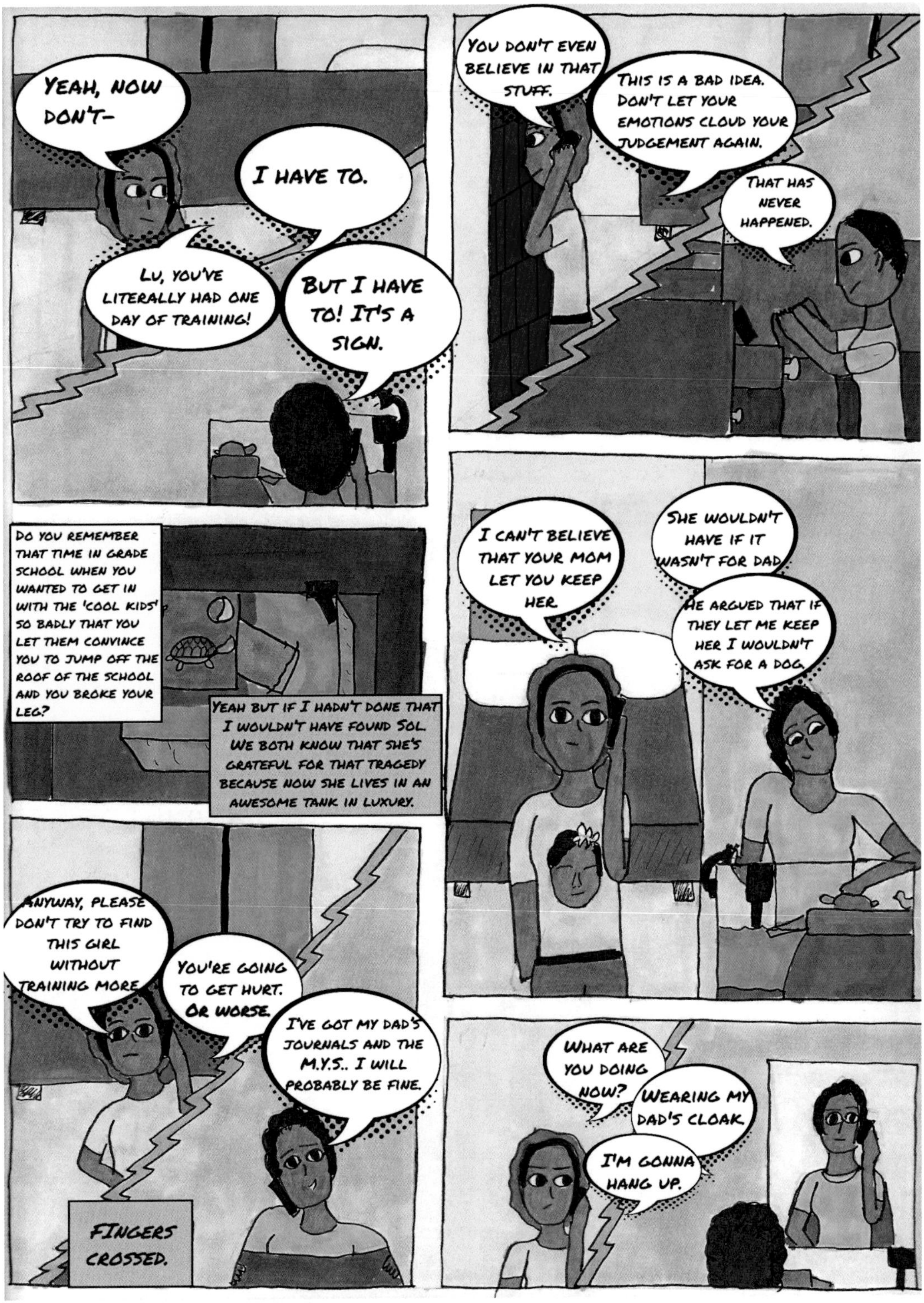
YEAH, NOW DON'T-
I HAVE TO.
LU, YOU'VE LITERALLY HAD ONE DAY OF TRAINING!
BUT I HAVE TO! IT'S A SIGN.
YOU DON'T EVEN BELIEVE IN THAT STUFF.
THIS IS A BAD IDEA. DON'T LET YOUR EMOTIONS CLOUD YOUR JUDGEMENT AGAIN.
THAT HAS NEVER HAPPENED.
DO YOU REMEMBER THAT TIME IN GRADE SCHOOL WHEN YOU WANTED TO GET IN WITH THE 'COOL KIDS' SO BADLY THAT YOU LET THEM CONVINCE YOU TO JUMP OFF THE ROOF OF THE SCHOOL AND YOU BROKE YOUR LEG?
YEAH BUT IF I HADN'T DONE THAT I WOULDN'T HAVE FOUND SOL. WE BOTH KNOW THAT SHE'S GRATEFUL FOR THAT TRAGEDY BECAUSE NOW SHE LIVES IN AN AWESOME TANK IN LUXURY.
I CAN'T BELIEVE THAT YOUR MOM LET YOU KEEP HER.
SHE WOULDN'T HAVE IF IT WASN'T FOR DAD.
HE ARGUED THAT IF THEY LET ME KEEP HER I WOULDN'T ASK FOR A DOG.
ANYWAY, PLEASE DON'T TRY TO FIND THIS GIRL WITHOUT TRAINING MORE.
YOU'RE GOING TO GET HURT. OR WORSE.
I'VE GOT MY DAD'S JOURNALS AND THE M.Y.S.. I WILL PROBABLY BE FINE.
FINGERS CROSSED.
WHAT ARE YOU DOING NOW?
WEARING MY DAD'S CLOAK.
I'M GONNA HANG UP.

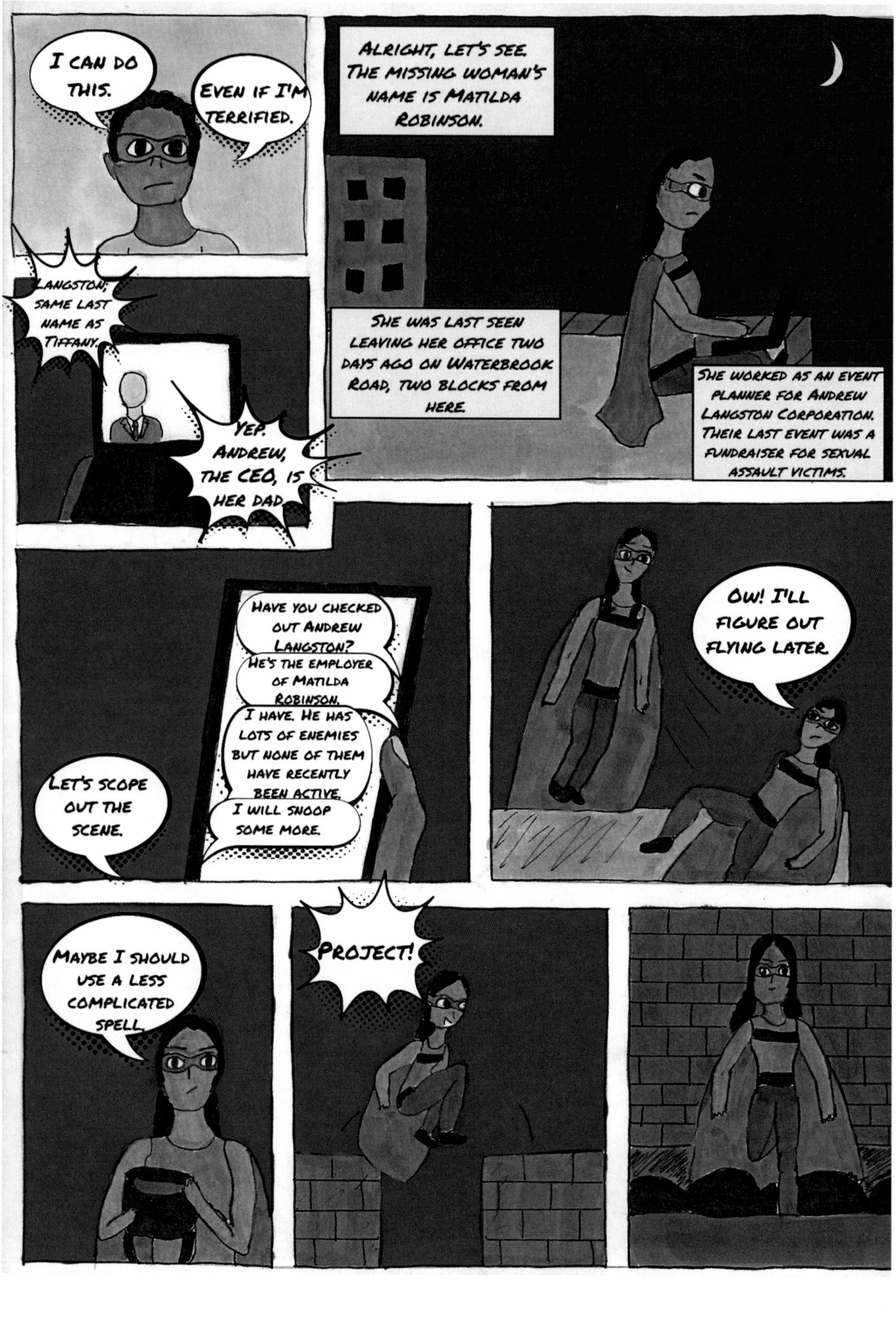
I can do this.
Even if I'm terrified.
Alright, let's see. The missing woman's name is Matilda Robinson.
She was last seen leaving her office two days ago on Waterbrook Road, two blocks from here.
She worked as an event planner for Andrew Langston Corporation. Their last event was a fundraiser for sexual assault victims.
Langston; same last name as Tiffany.
Yep. Andrew, the CEO, is her dad.
Have you checked out Andrew Langston?
He's the employer of Matilda Robinson.
I have. He has lots of enemies but none of them have recently been active.
I will snoop some more.
Let's scope out the scene.
Ow! I'll figure out flying later.
Maybe I should use a less complicated spell.
Project!

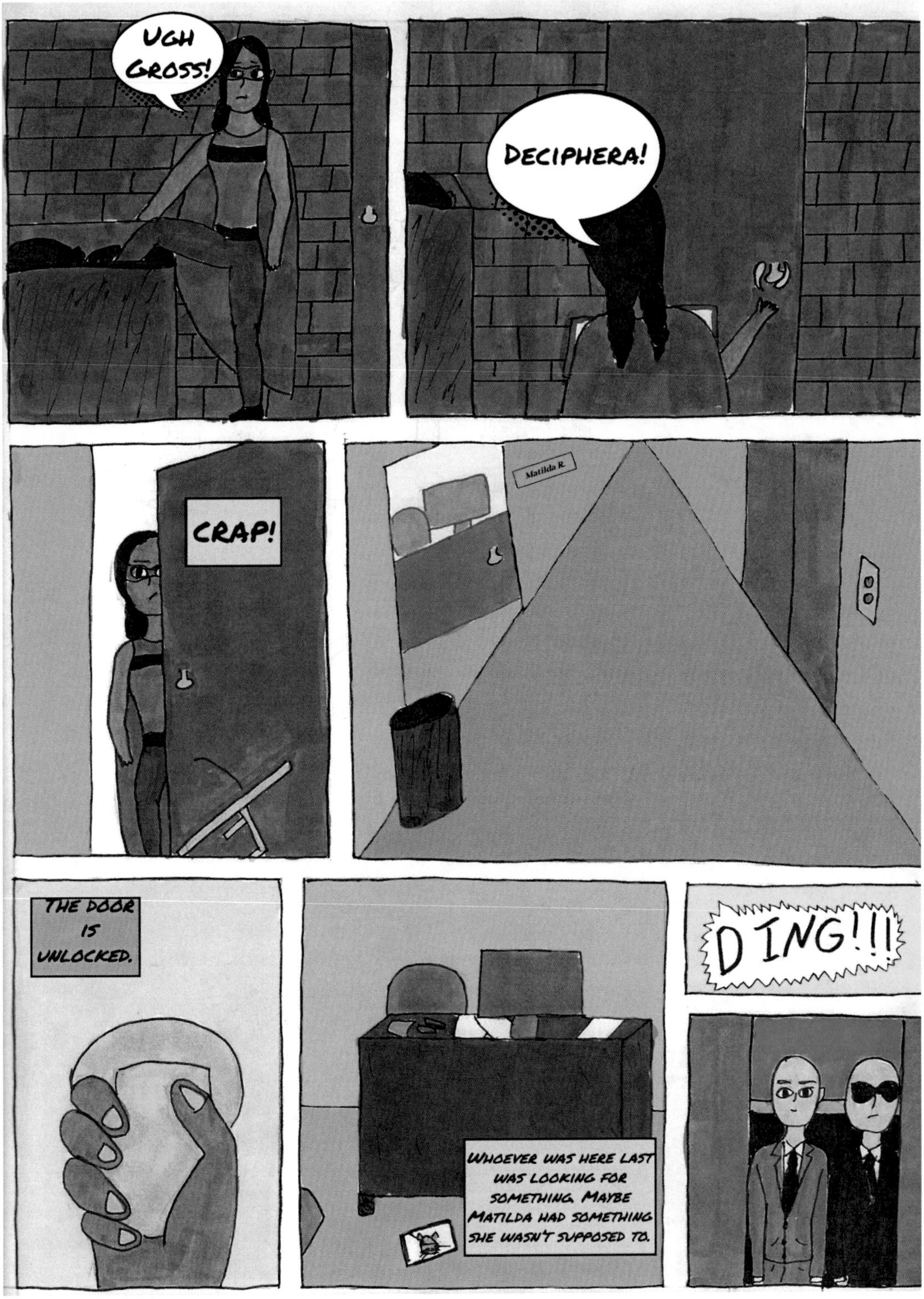
UGH GROSS!
DECIPHERA!
CRAP!
Matilda R.
THE DOOR IS UNLOCKED.
WHOEVER WAS HERE LAST WAS LOOKING FOR SOMETHING. MAYBE MATILDA HAD SOMETHING SHE WASN'T SUPPOSED TO.
DING!!!

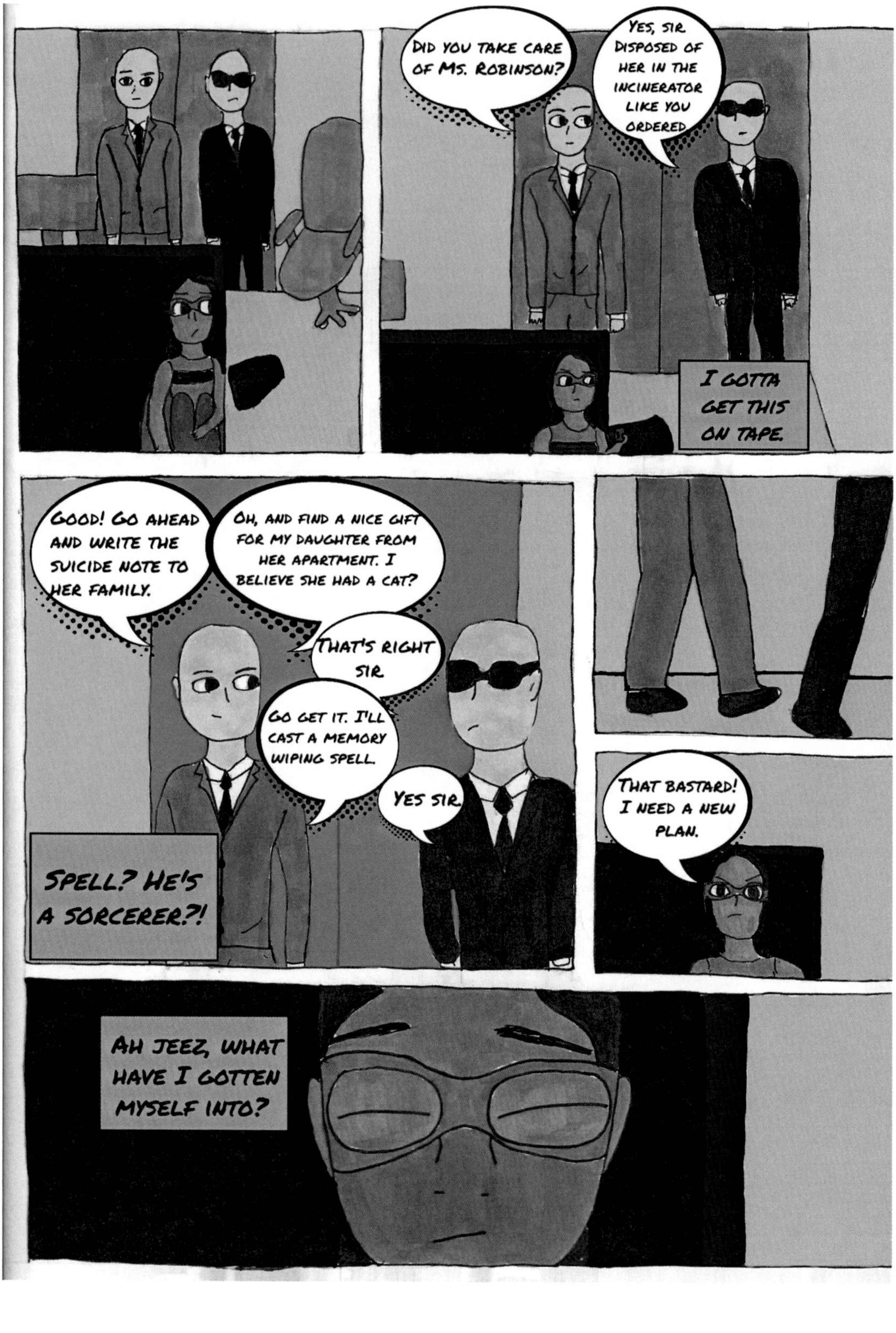
Did you take care of Ms. Robinson?
Yes, sir. Disposed of her in the incinerator like you ordered.
I gotta get this on tape.
Good! Go ahead and write the suicide note to her family.
Oh, and find a nice gift for my daughter from her apartment. I believe she had a cat?
That's right sir.
Go get it. I'll cast a memory wiping spell.
Yes sir.
Spell? He's a sorcerer?!
That bastard! I need a new plan.
Ah jeez, what have I gotten myself into?

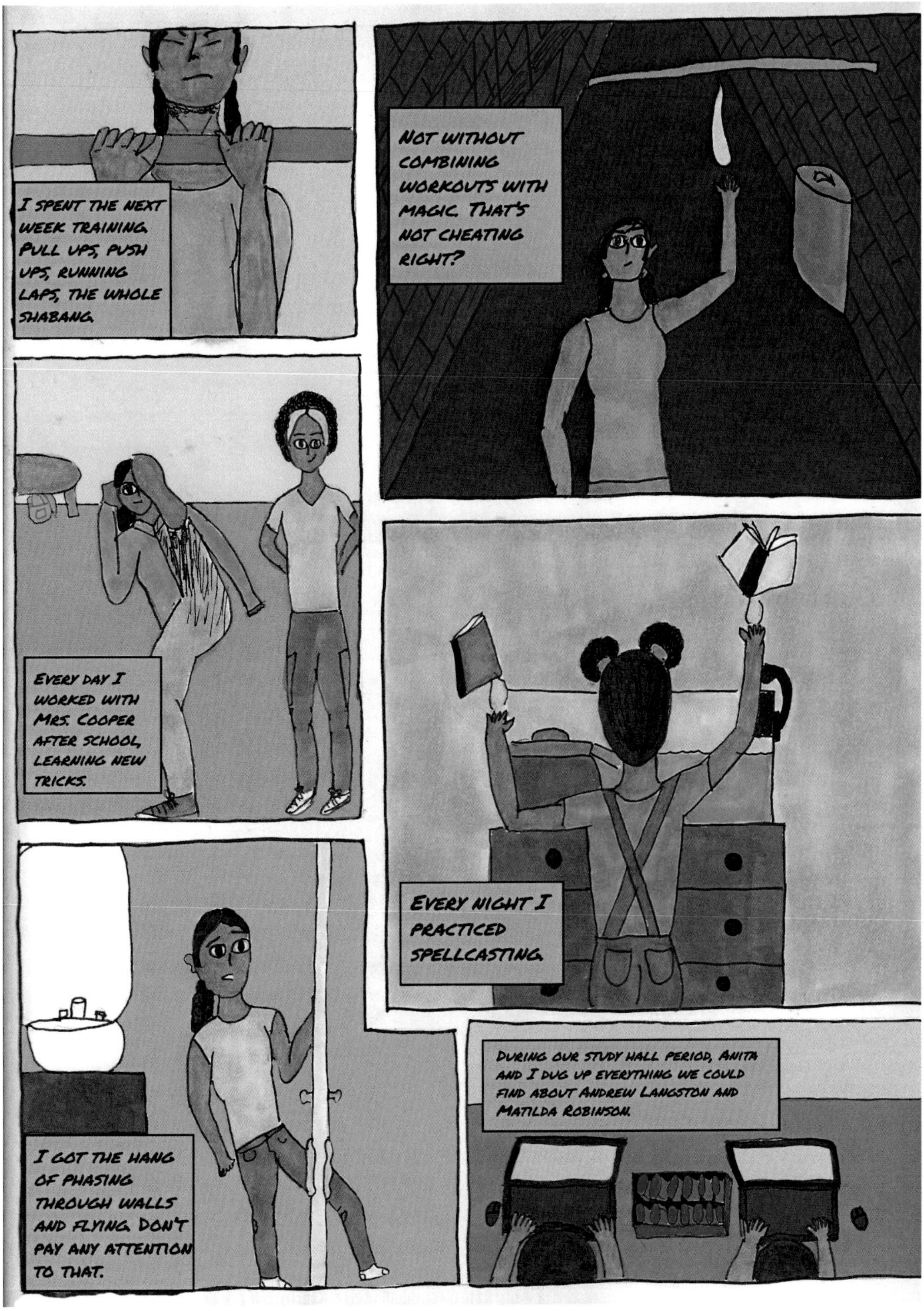
I SPENT THE NEXT WEEK TRAINING. PULL UPS, PUSH UPS, RUNNING LAPS, THE WHOLE SHABANG.
NOT WITHOUT COMBINING WORKOUTS WITH MAGIC. THAT'S NOT CHEATING RIGHT?
EVERY DAY I WORKED WITH MRS. COOPER AFTER SCHOOL, LEARNING NEW TRICKS.
EVERY NIGHT I PRACTICED SPELLCASTING.
I GOT THE HANG OF PHASING THROUGH WALLS AND FLYING. DON'T PAY ANY ATTENTION TO THAT.
DURING OUR STUDY HALL PERIOD, ANITA AND I DUG UP EVERYTHING WE COULD FIND ABOUT ANDREW LANGSTON AND MATILDA ROBINSON.

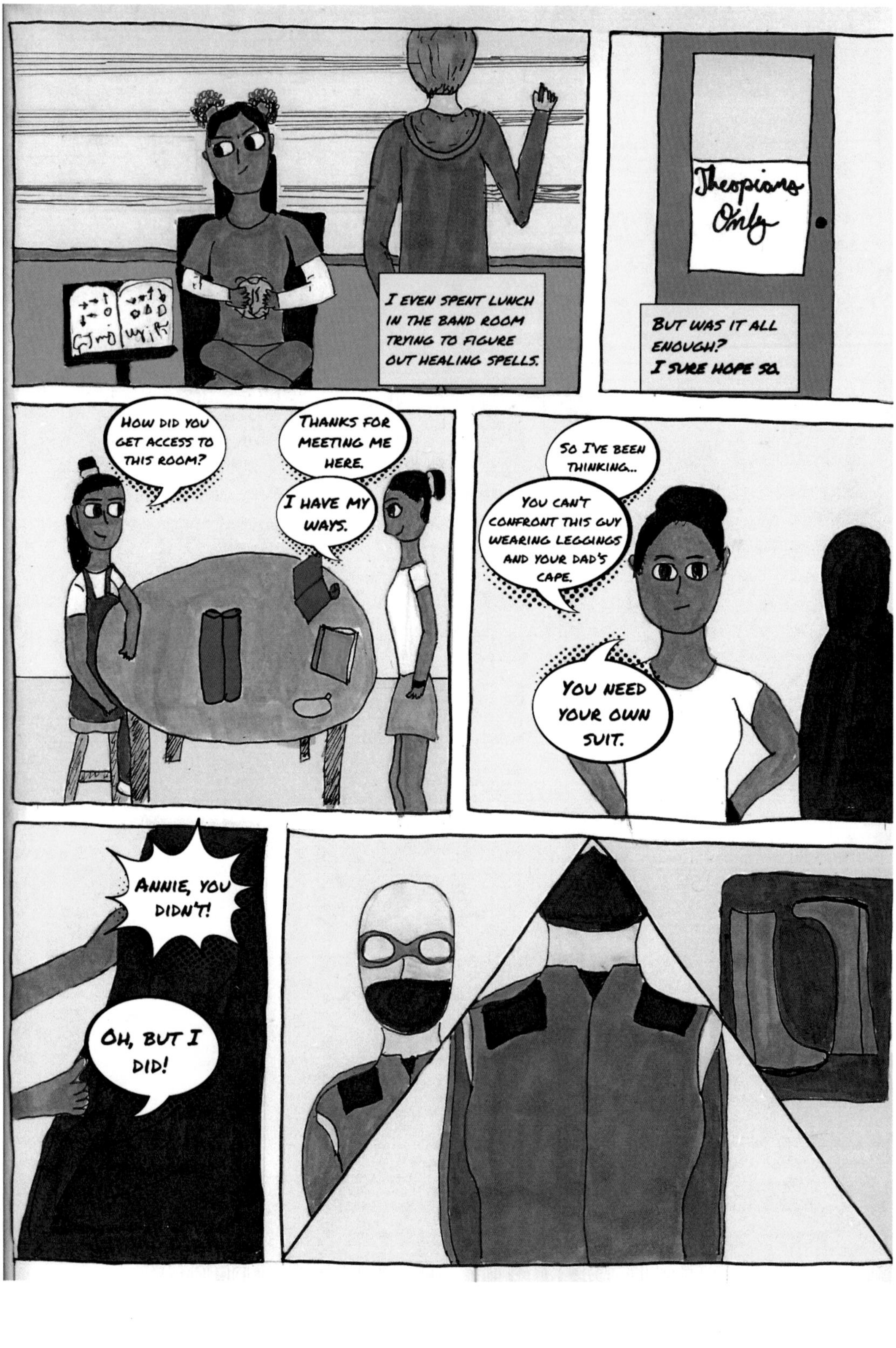
I EVEN SPENT LUNCH IN THE BAND ROOM TRYING TO FIGURE OUT HEALING SPELLS.
Thespians Only
BUT WAS IT ALL ENOUGH? I SURE HOPE SO.
HOW DID YOU GET ACCESS TO THIS ROOM?
THANKS FOR MEETING ME HERE.
I HAVE MY WAYS.
SO I'VE BEEN THINKING...
YOU CAN'T CONFRONT THIS GUY WEARING LEGGINGS AND YOUR DAD'S CAPE.
YOU NEED YOUR OWN SUIT.
ANNIE, YOU DIDN'T!
OH, BUT I DID!

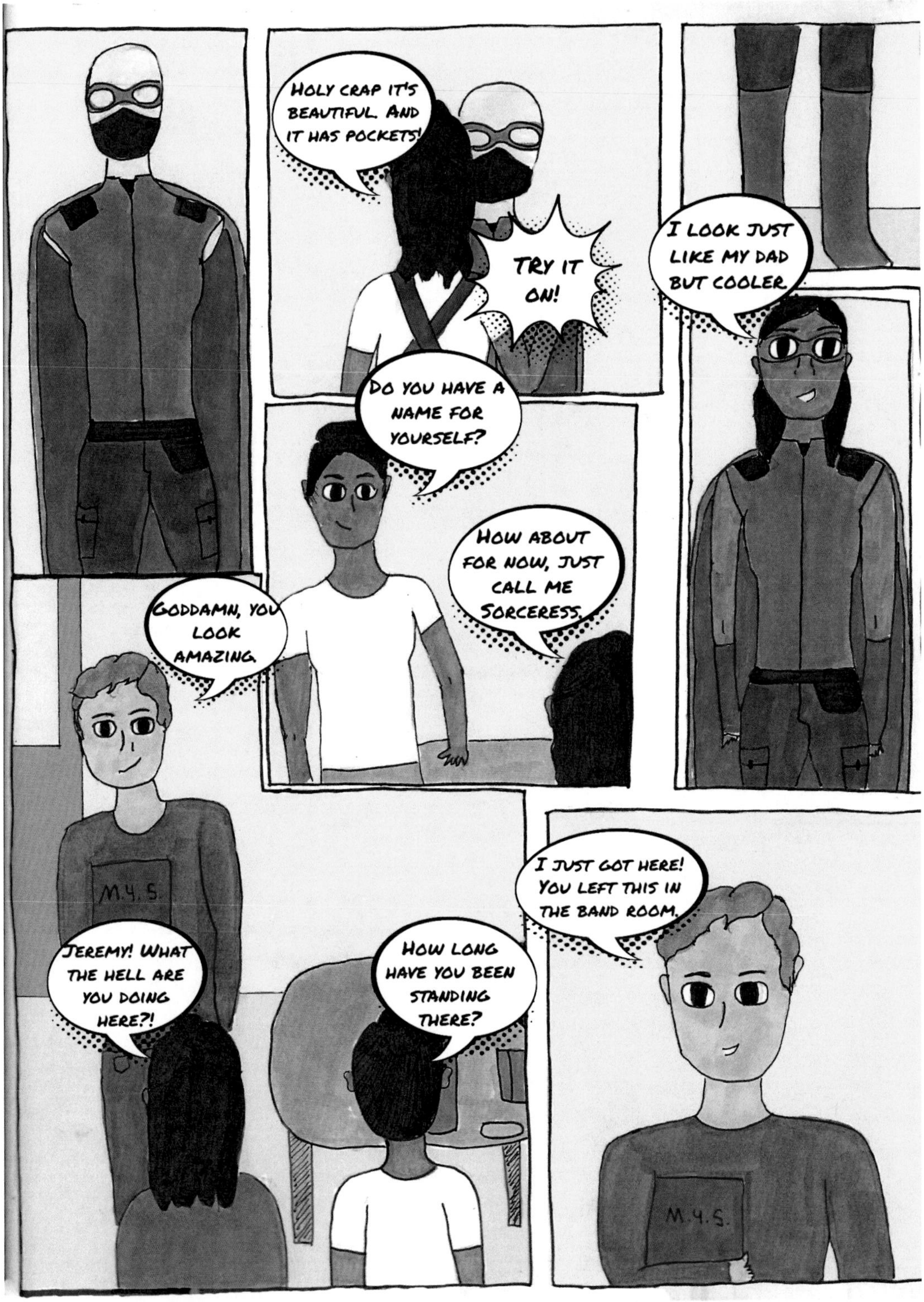
Holy crap it's beautiful. And it has pockets!
Try it on!
I look just like my dad but cooler.
Do you have a name for yourself?
How about for now, just call me Sorceress.
Goddamn, you look amazing.
M.Y.S.
Jeremy! What the hell are you doing here?!
How long have you been standing there?
I just got here! You left this in the band room.
M.Y.S.

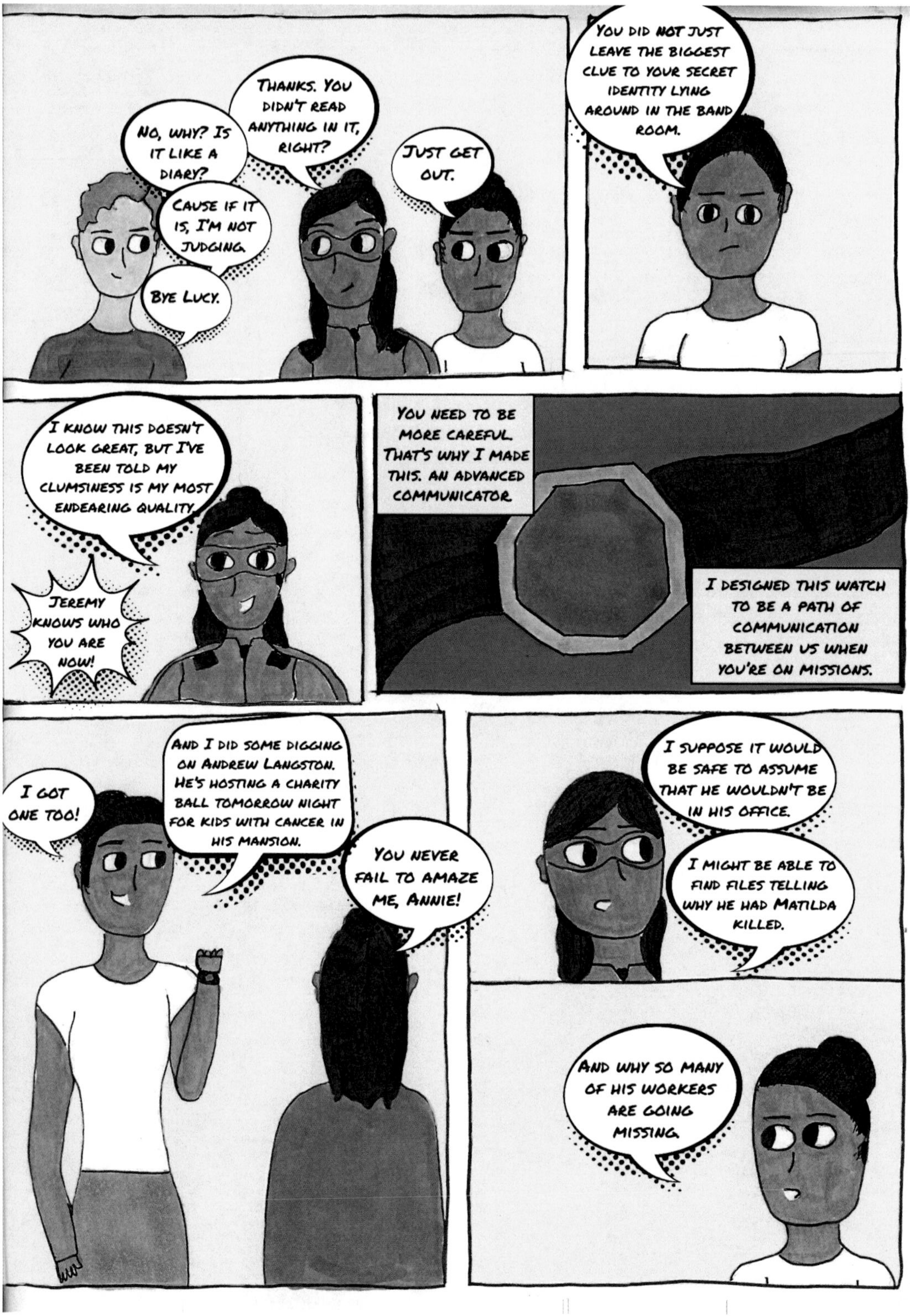
No, why? Is it like a diary?
Thanks. You didn't read anything in it, right?
Cause if it is, I'm not judging.
Bye Lucy.
Just get out.
You did not just leave the biggest clue to your secret identity lying around in the band room.
I know this doesn't look great, but I've been told my clumsiness is my most endearing quality.
Jeremy knows who you are now!
You need to be more careful. That's why I made this. An advanced communicator.
I designed this watch to be a path of communication between us when you're on missions.
I got one too!
And I did some digging on Andrew Langston. He's hosting a charity ball tomorrow night for kids with cancer in his mansion.
You never fail to amaze me, Annie!
I suppose it would be safe to assume that he wouldn't be in his office.
I might be able to find files telling why he had Matilda killed.
And why so many of his workers are going missing.

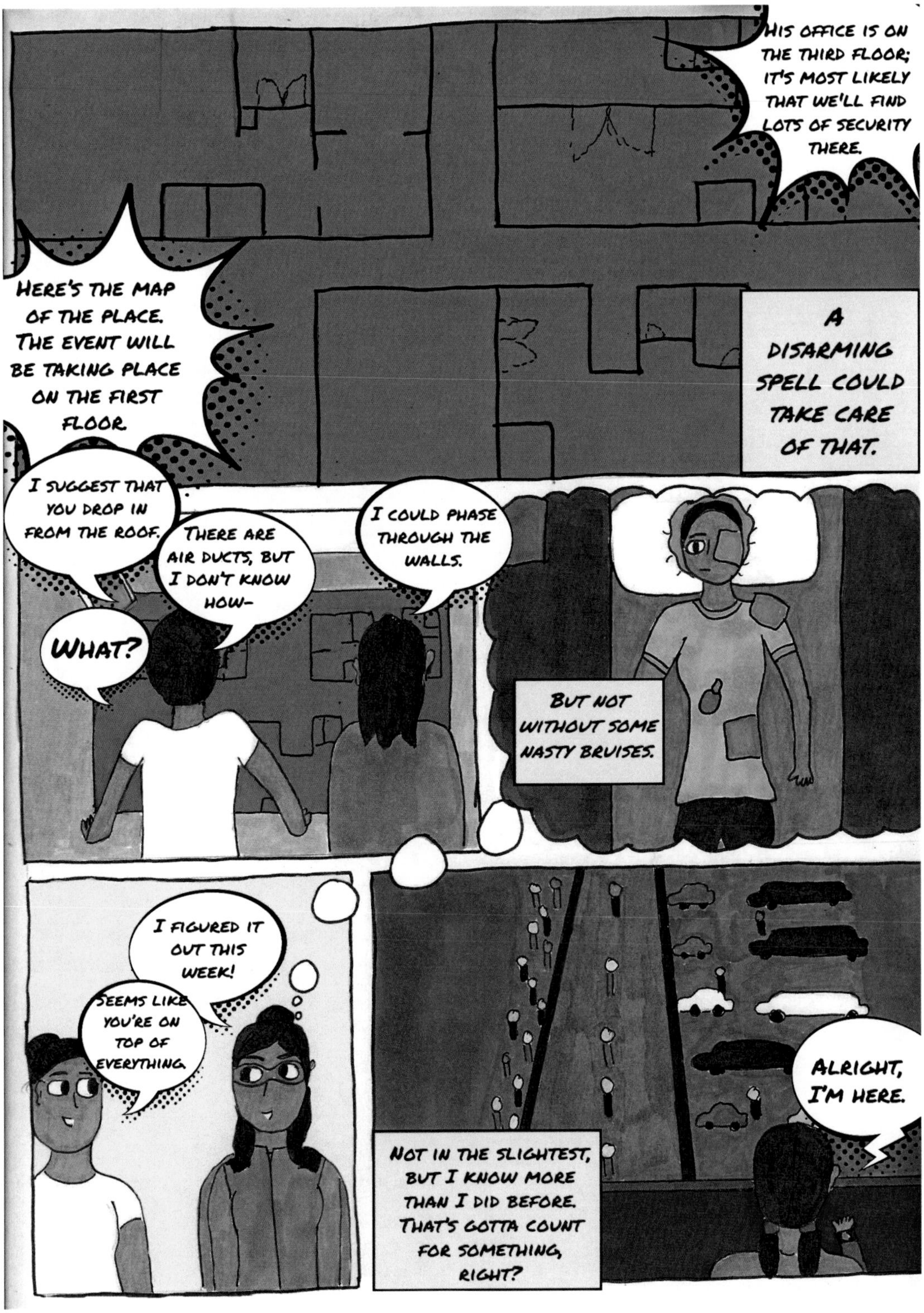
Here's the map of the place. The event will be taking place on the first floor.
His office is on the third floor; it's most likely that we'll find lots of security there.
A disarming spell could take care of that.
I suggest that you drop in from the roof.
What?
There are air ducts, but I don't know how-
I could phase through the walls.
But not without some nasty bruises.
Seems like you're on top of everything.
I figured it out this week!
Not in the slightest, but I know more than I did before. That's gotta count for something, right?
Alright, I'm here.

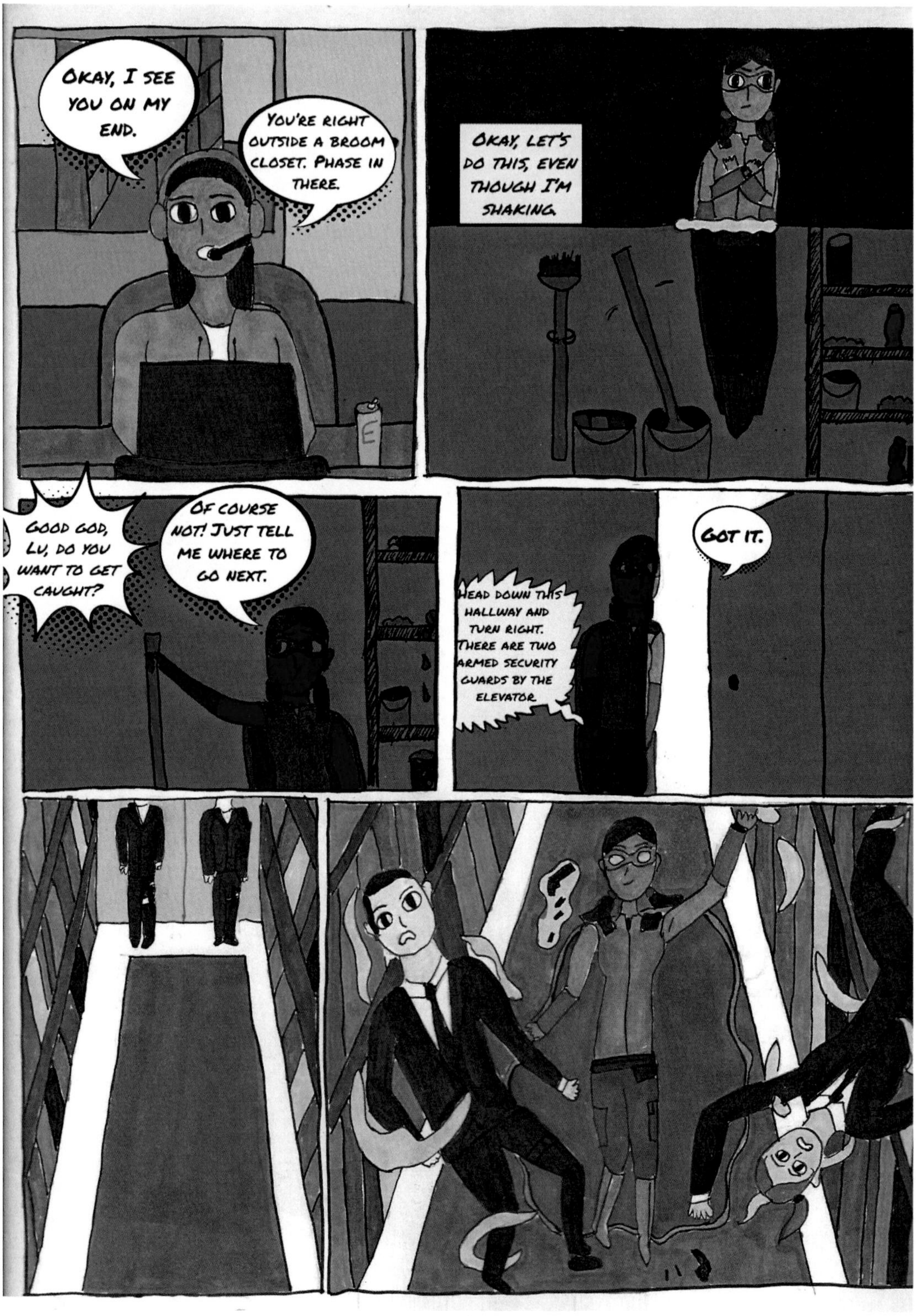
Okay, I see you on my end.
You're right outside a broom closet. Phase in there.
Okay, let's do this, even though I'm shaking.
Good god, Lu, do you want to get caught?
Of course not! Just tell me where to go next.
Head down this hallway and turn right. There are two armed security guards by the elevator.
Got it.

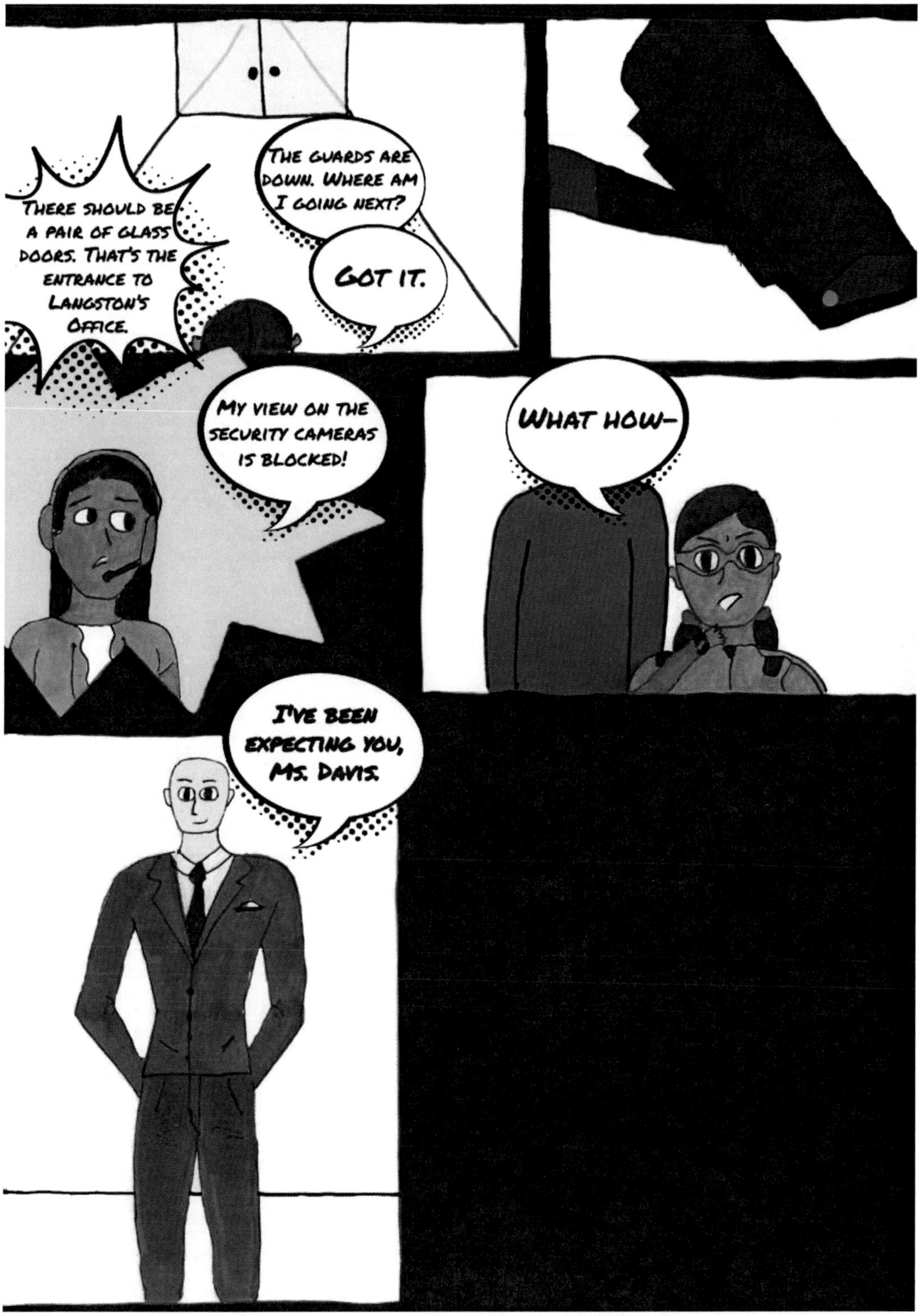
The guards are down. Where am I going next?
There should be a pair of glass doors. That's the entrance to Langston's Office.
Got it.
My view on the security cameras is blocked!
What how-
I've been expecting you, Ms. Davis.

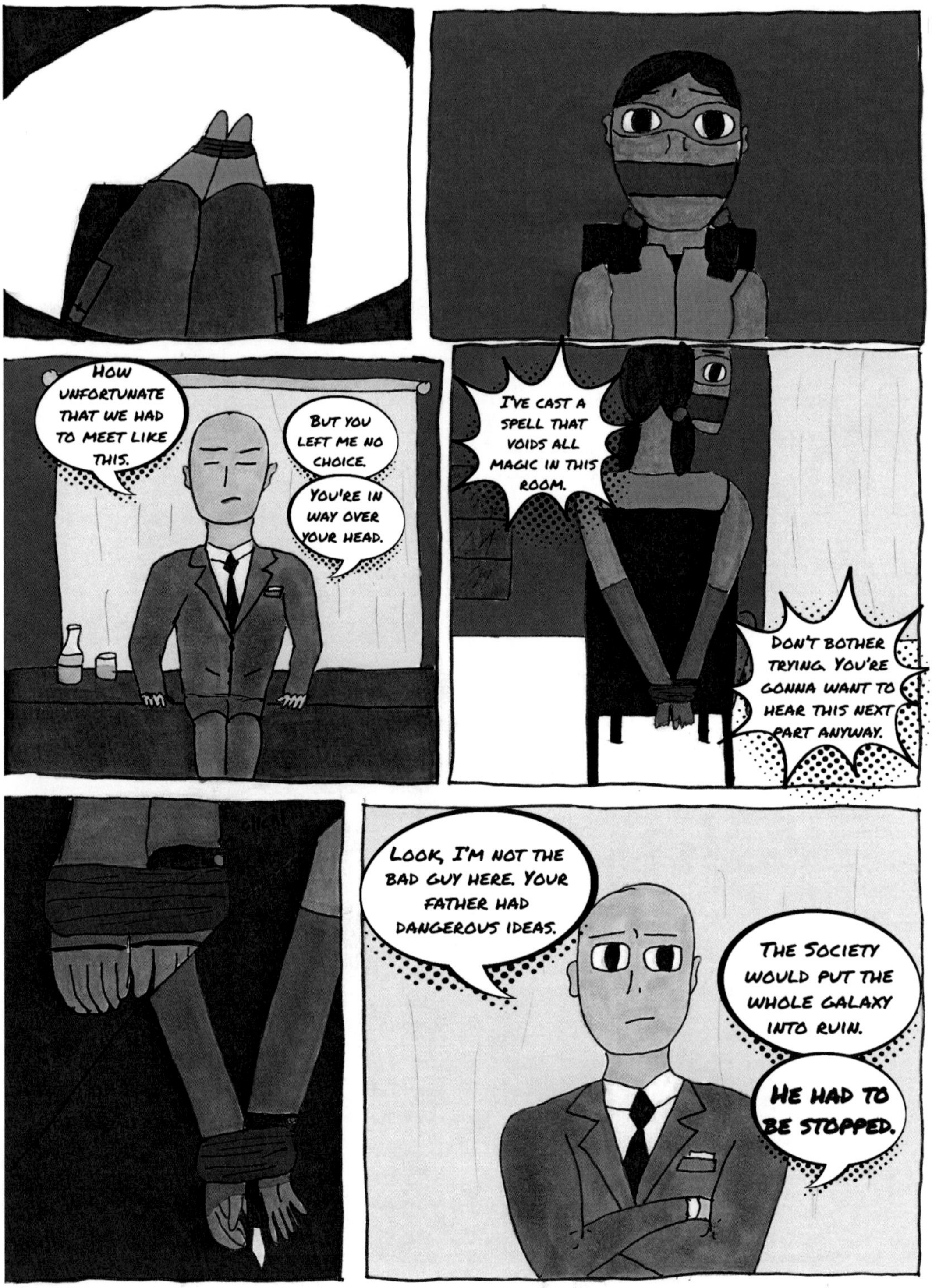
How unfortunate that we had to meet like this.
But you left me no choice.
You're in way over your head.
I've cast a spell that voids all magic in this room.
Don't bother trying. You're gonna want to hear this next part anyway.
Look, I'm not the bad guy here. Your father had dangerous ideas.
The Society would put the whole galaxy into ruin.
He had to be stopped.

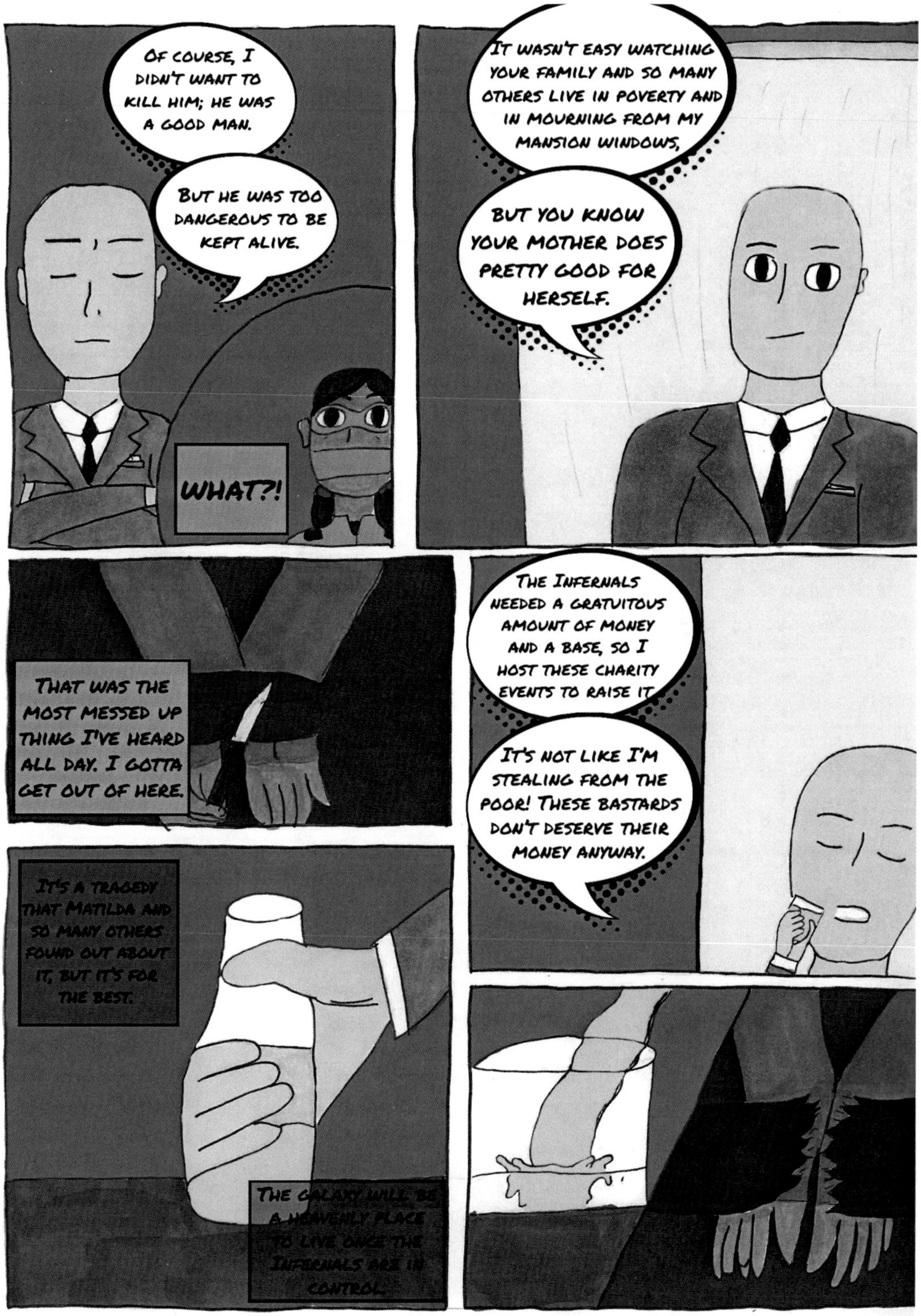

Of course, I didn't want to kill him; he was a good man.
But he was too dangerous to be kept alive.
WHAT?!
It wasn't easy watching your family and so many others live in poverty and in mourning from my mansion windows,
But you know your mother does pretty good for herself.
That was the most messed up thing I've heard all day. I gotta get out of here.
The Infernals needed a gratuitous amount of money and a base, so I host these charity events to raise it.
It's not like I'm stealing from the poor! These bastards don't deserve their money anyway.
It's a tragedy that Matilda and so many others found out about it, but it's for the best.
The galaxy will be a heavenly place to live once the Infernals are in control.

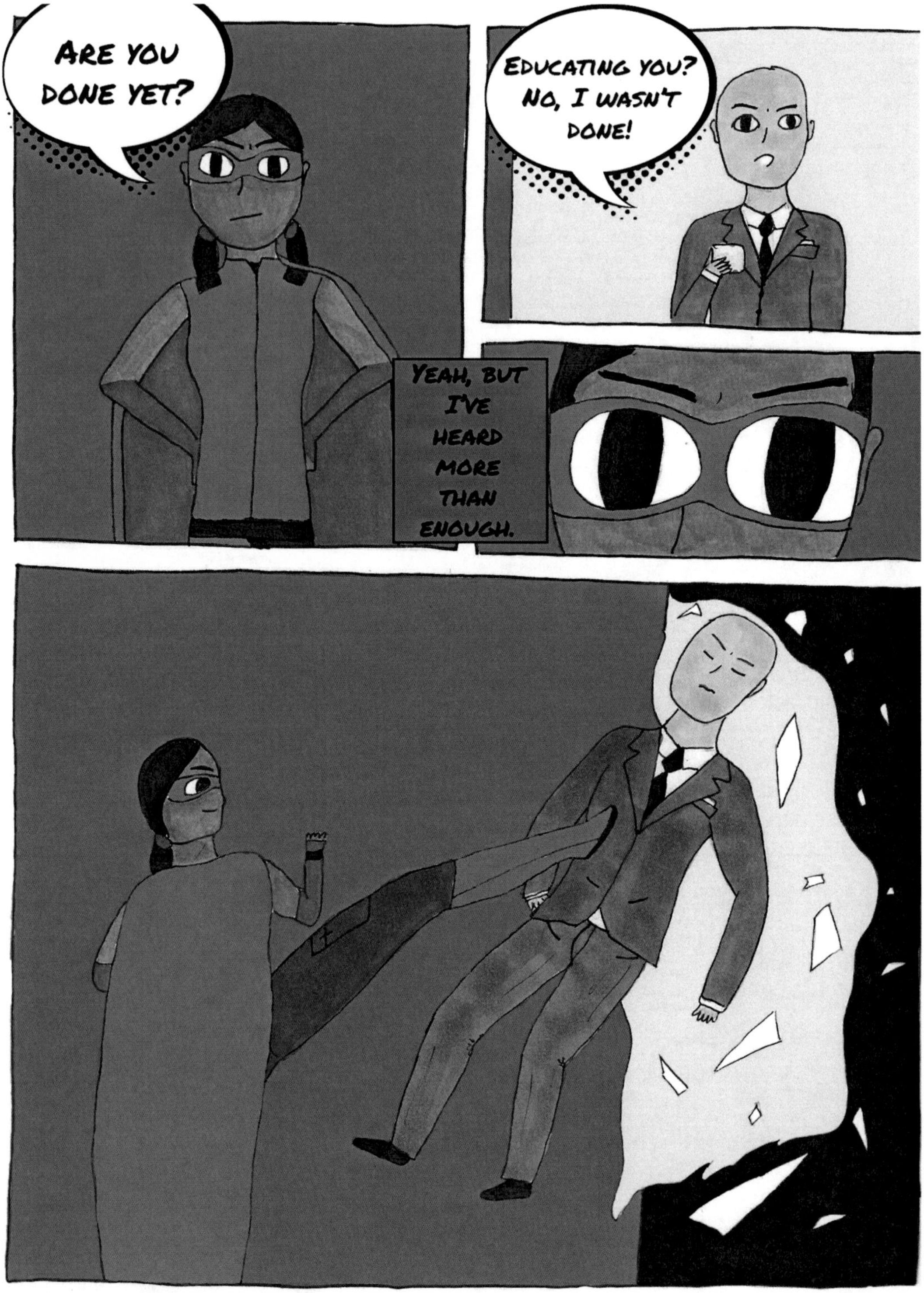
ARE YOU DONE YET?
EDUCATING YOU? NO, I WASN'T DONE!
YEAH, BUT I'VE HEARD MORE THAN ENOUGH.

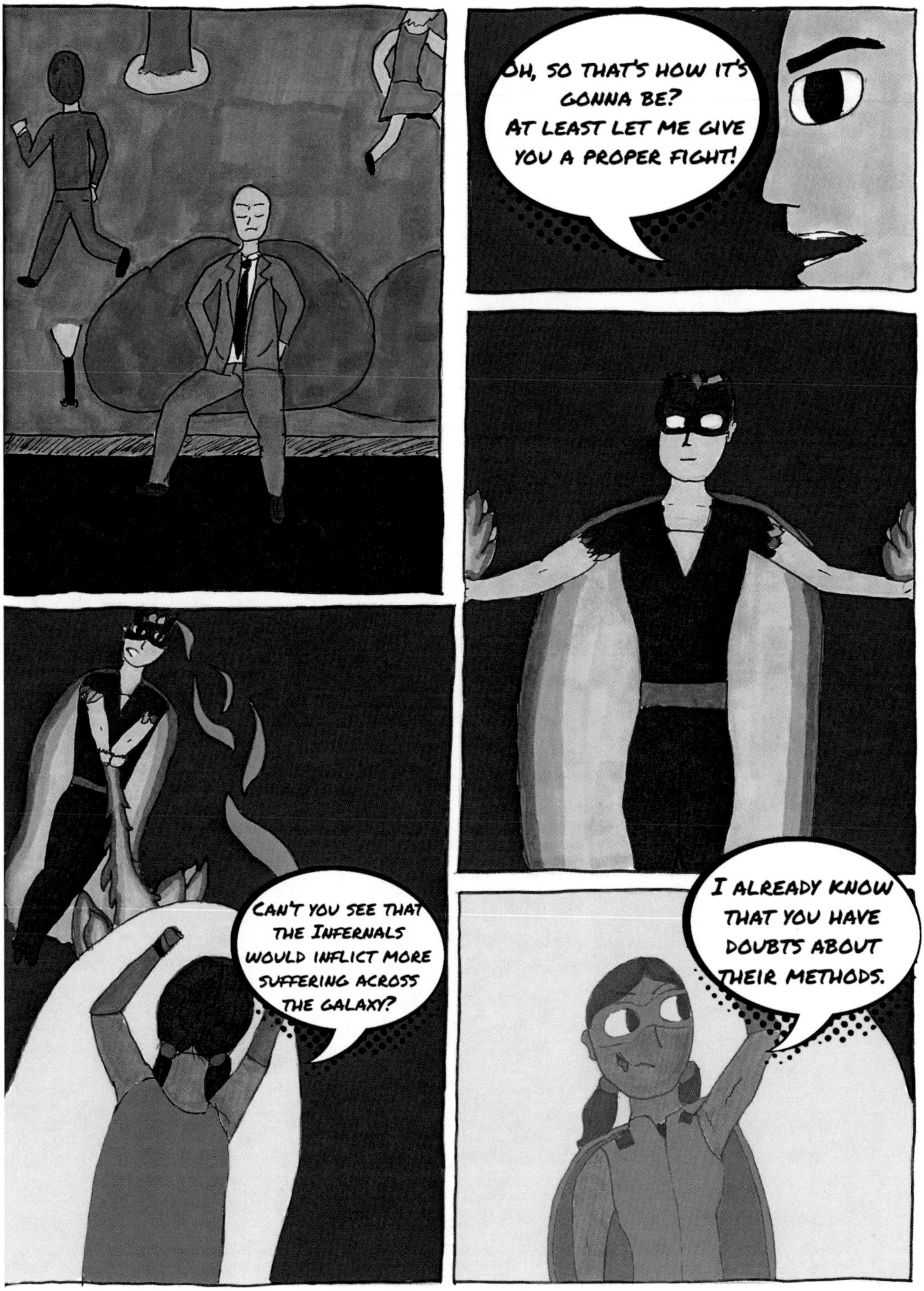
Oh, so that's how it's gonna be? At least let me give you a proper fight!
Can't you see that the Infernals would inflict more suffering across the galaxy?
I already know that you have doubts about their methods.

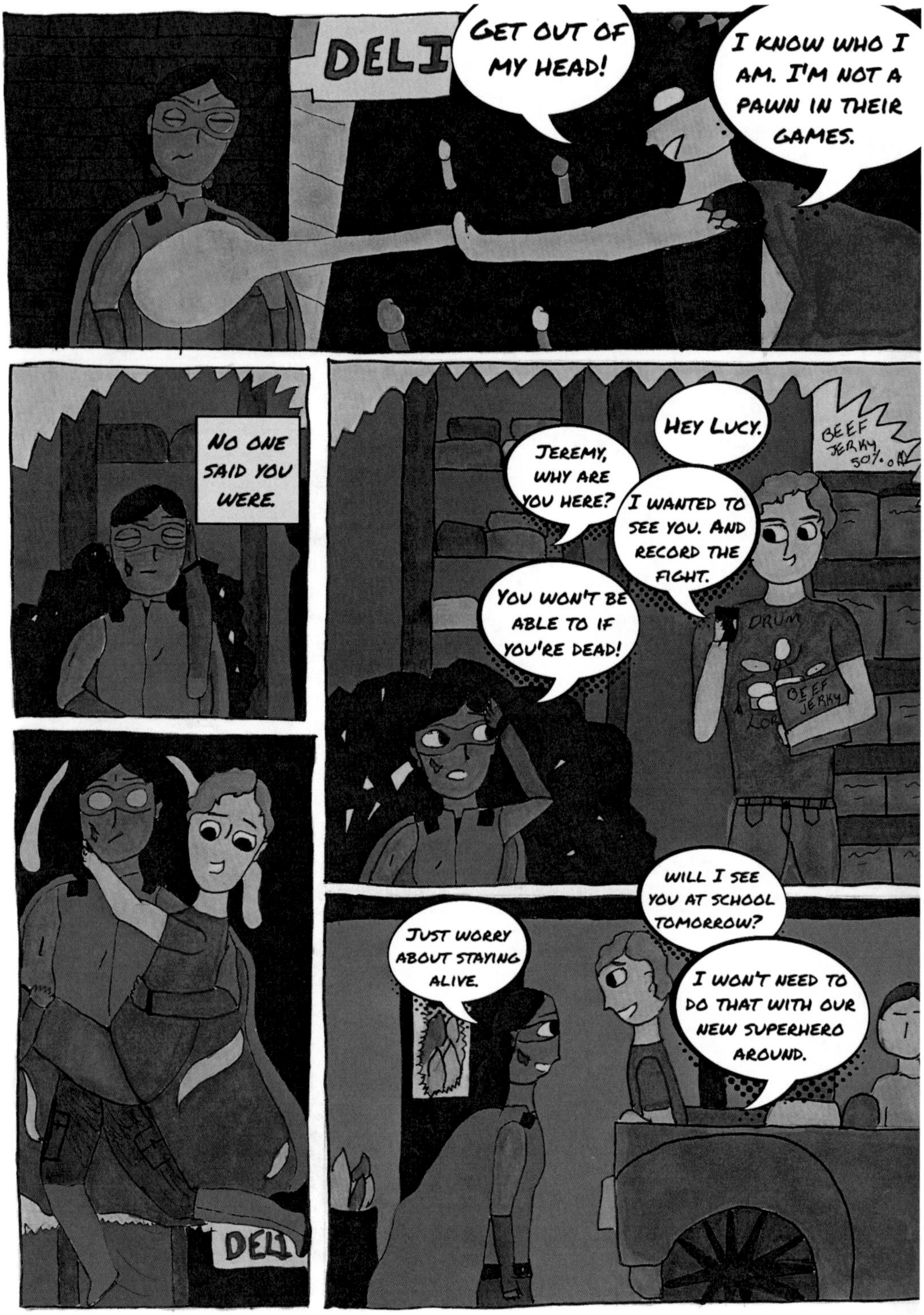
DELI
GET OUT OF MY HEAD!
I KNOW WHO I AM. I'M NOT A PAWN IN THEIR GAMES.
NO ONE SAID YOU WERE.
HEY LUCY.
BEEF JERKY 50% OFF
JEREMY, WHY ARE YOU HERE?
I WANTED TO SEE YOU. AND RECORD THE FIGHT.
YOU WON'T BE ABLE TO IF YOU'RE DEAD!
DRUM
BEEF JERKY
DELI
WILL I SEE YOU AT SCHOOL TOMORROW?
JUST WORRY ABOUT STAYING ALIVE.
I WON'T NEED TO DO THAT WITH OUR NEW SUPERHERO AROUND.

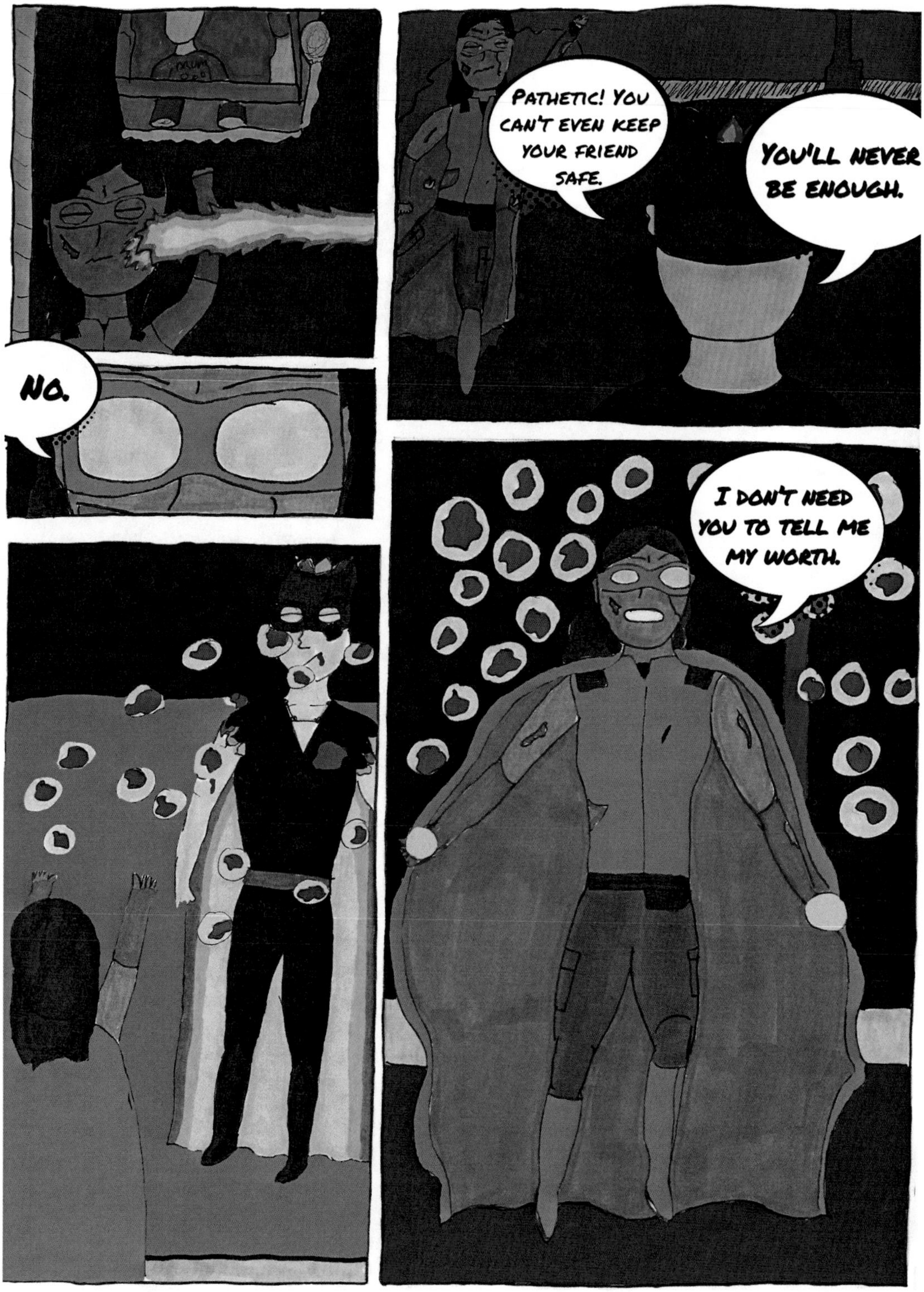
PATHETIC! YOU CAN'T EVEN KEEP YOUR FRIEND SAFE.
YOU'LL NEVER BE ENOUGH.
NO.
I DON'T NEED YOU TO TELL ME MY WORTH.

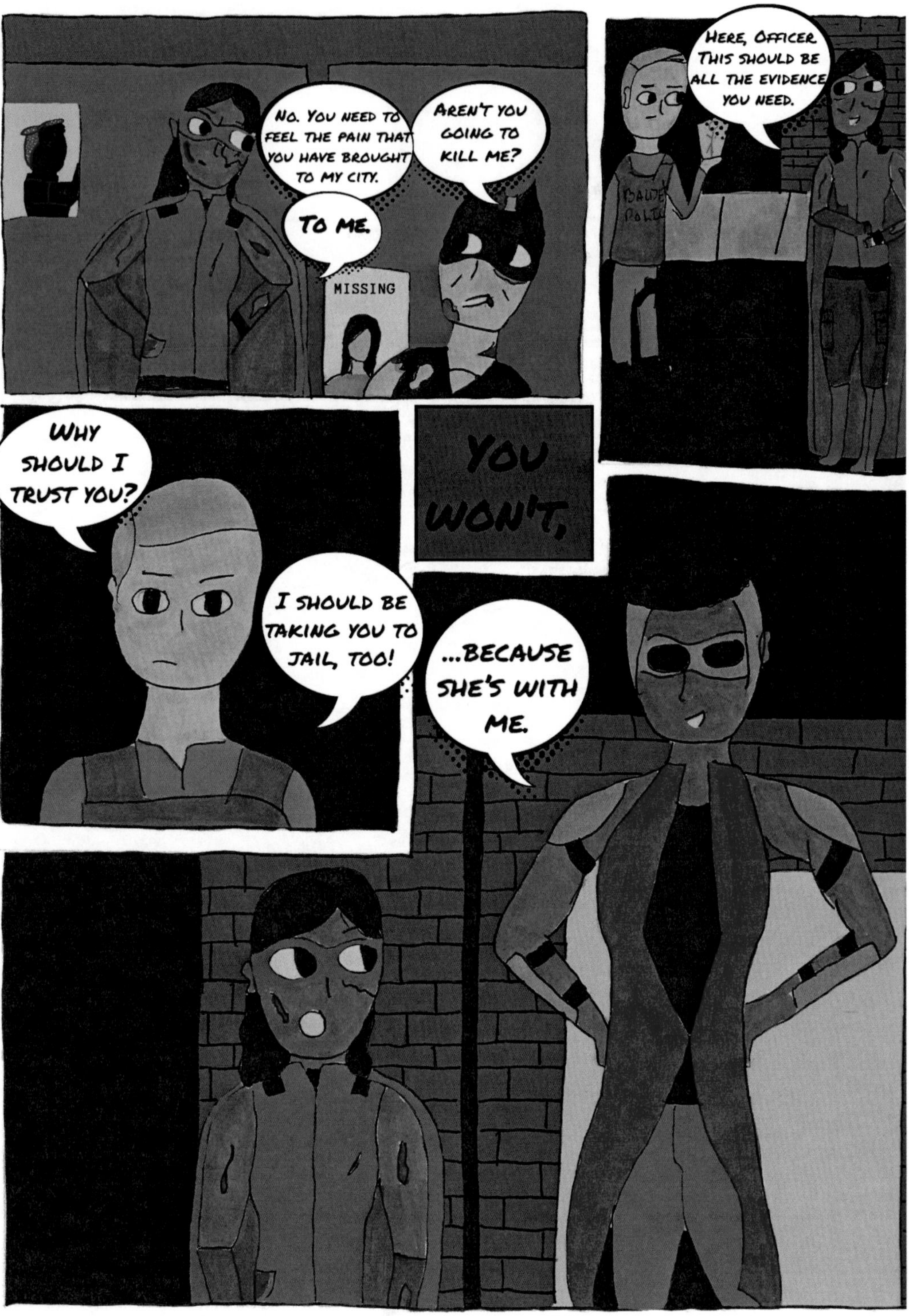
No. You need to feel the pain that you have brought to my city.
Aren't you going to kill me?
To me.
MISSING
Here, Officer. This should be all the evidence you need.
Why should I trust you?
I should be taking you to jail, too!
You won't,
...because she's with me.

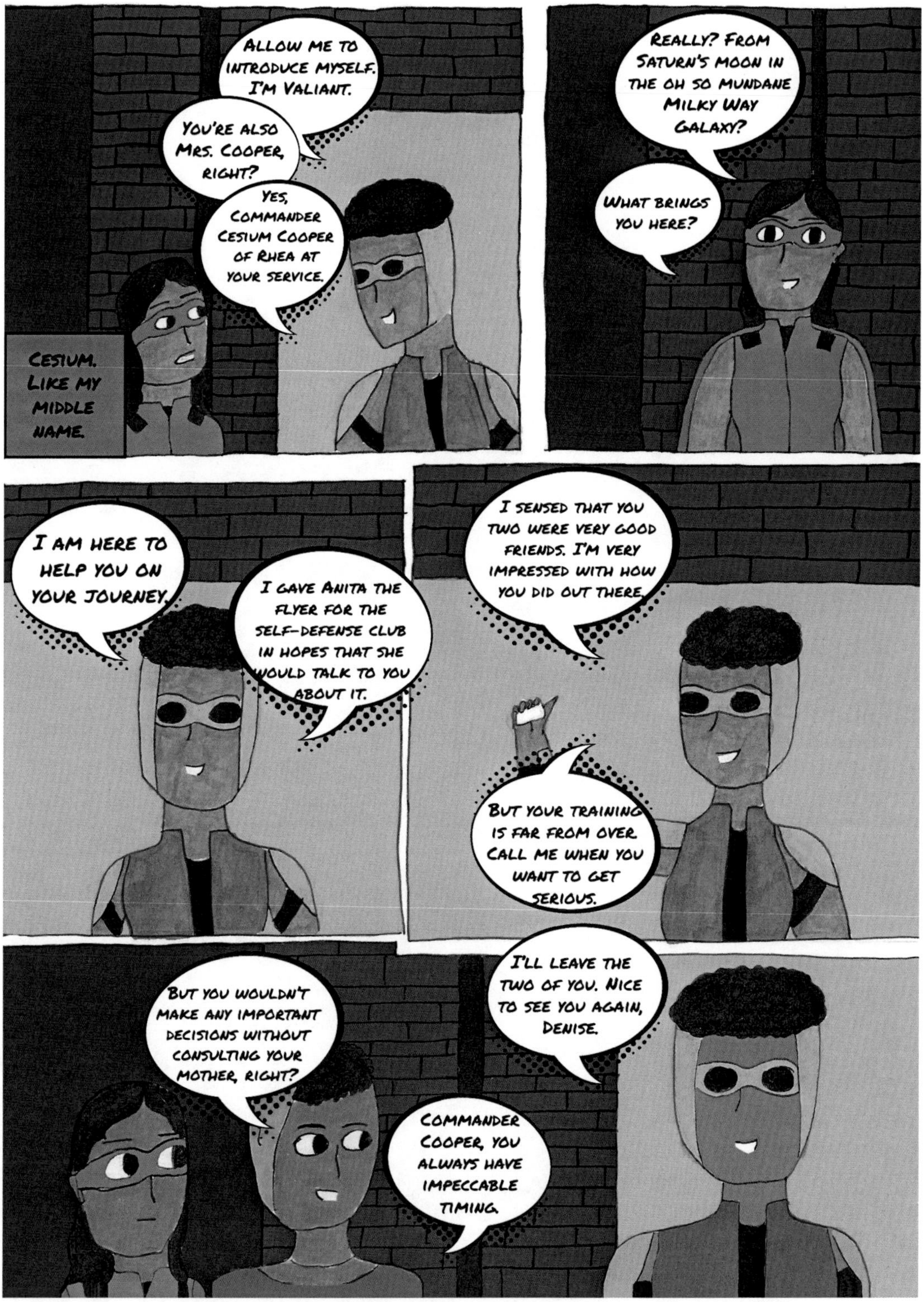

Allow me to introduce myself. I'm Valiant.
You're also Mrs. Cooper, right?
Yes, Commander Cesium Cooper of Rhea at your service.
Cesium. Like my middle name.
Really? From Saturn's moon in the oh so mundane Milky Way Galaxy?
What brings you here?
I am here to help you on your journey.
I gave Anita the flyer for the self-defense club in hopes that she would talk to you about it.
I sensed that you two were very good friends. I'm very impressed with how you did out there.
But your training is far from over. Call me when you want to get serious.
But you wouldn't make any important decisions without consulting your mother, right?
Commander Cooper, you always have impeccable timing.
I'll leave the two of you. Nice to see you again, Denise.

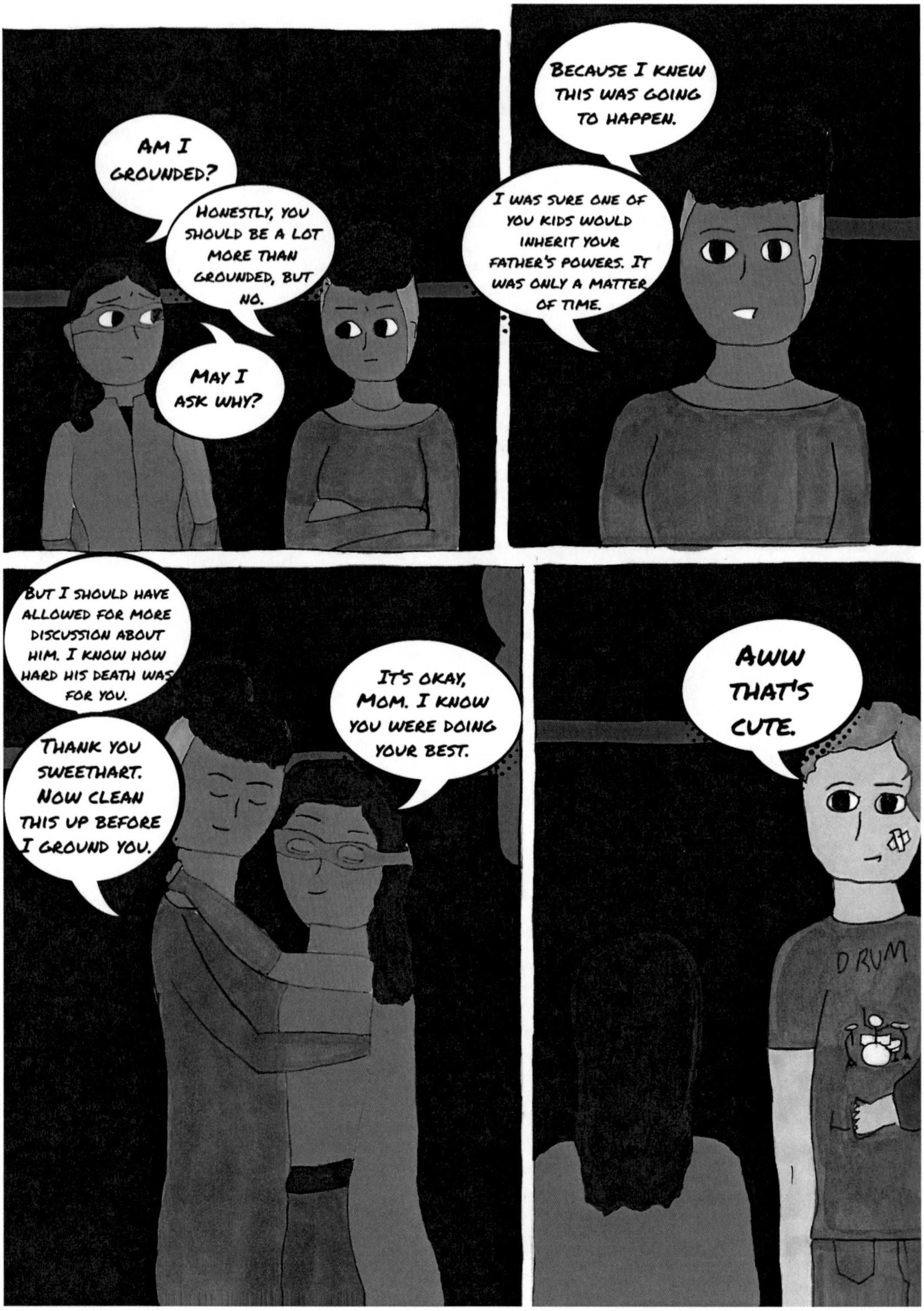
AM I GROUNDED?
HONESTLY, YOU SHOULD BE A LOT MORE THAN GROUNDED, BUT NO.
MAY I ASK WHY?
BECAUSE I KNEW THIS WAS GOING TO HAPPEN.
I WAS SURE ONE OF YOU KIDS WOULD INHERIT YOUR FATHER'S POWERS. IT WAS ONLY A MATTER OF TIME.
BUT I SHOULD HAVE ALLOWED FOR MORE DISCUSSION ABOUT HIM. I KNOW HOW HARD HIS DEATH WAS FOR YOU.
IT'S OKAY, MOM. I KNOW YOU WERE DOING YOUR BEST.
THANK YOU SWEETHART. NOW CLEAN THIS UP BEFORE I GROUND YOU.
AWW THAT'S CUTE.
DRUM

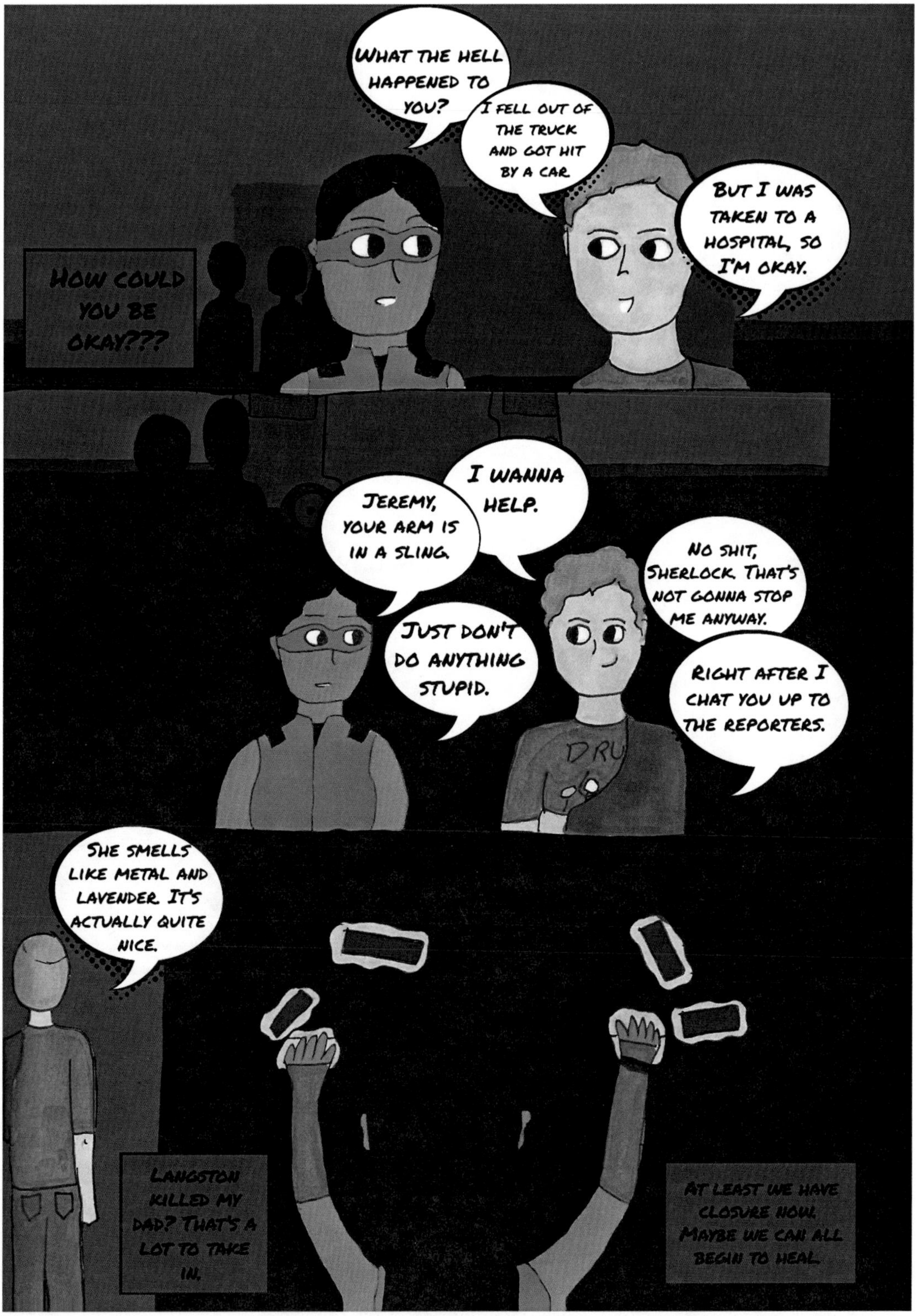
WHAT THE HELL HAPPENED TO YOU?
I FELL OUT OF THE TRUCK AND GOT HIT BY A CAR
BUT I WAS TAKEN TO A HOSPITAL, SO I'M OKAY.
HOW COULD YOU BE OKAY???
I WANNA HELP.
JEREMY, YOUR ARM IS IN A SLING.
NO SHIT, SHERLOCK. THAT'S NOT GONNA STOP ME ANYWAY.
JUST DON'T DO ANYTHING STUPID.
RIGHT AFTER I CHAT YOU UP TO THE REPORTERS.
SHE SMELLS LIKE METAL AND LAVENDER. IT'S ACTUALLY QUITE NICE.
LANGSTON KILLED MY DAD? THAT'S A LOT TO TAKE IN.
AT LEAST WE HAVE CLOSURE NOW. MAYBE WE CAN ALL BEGIN TO HEAL.

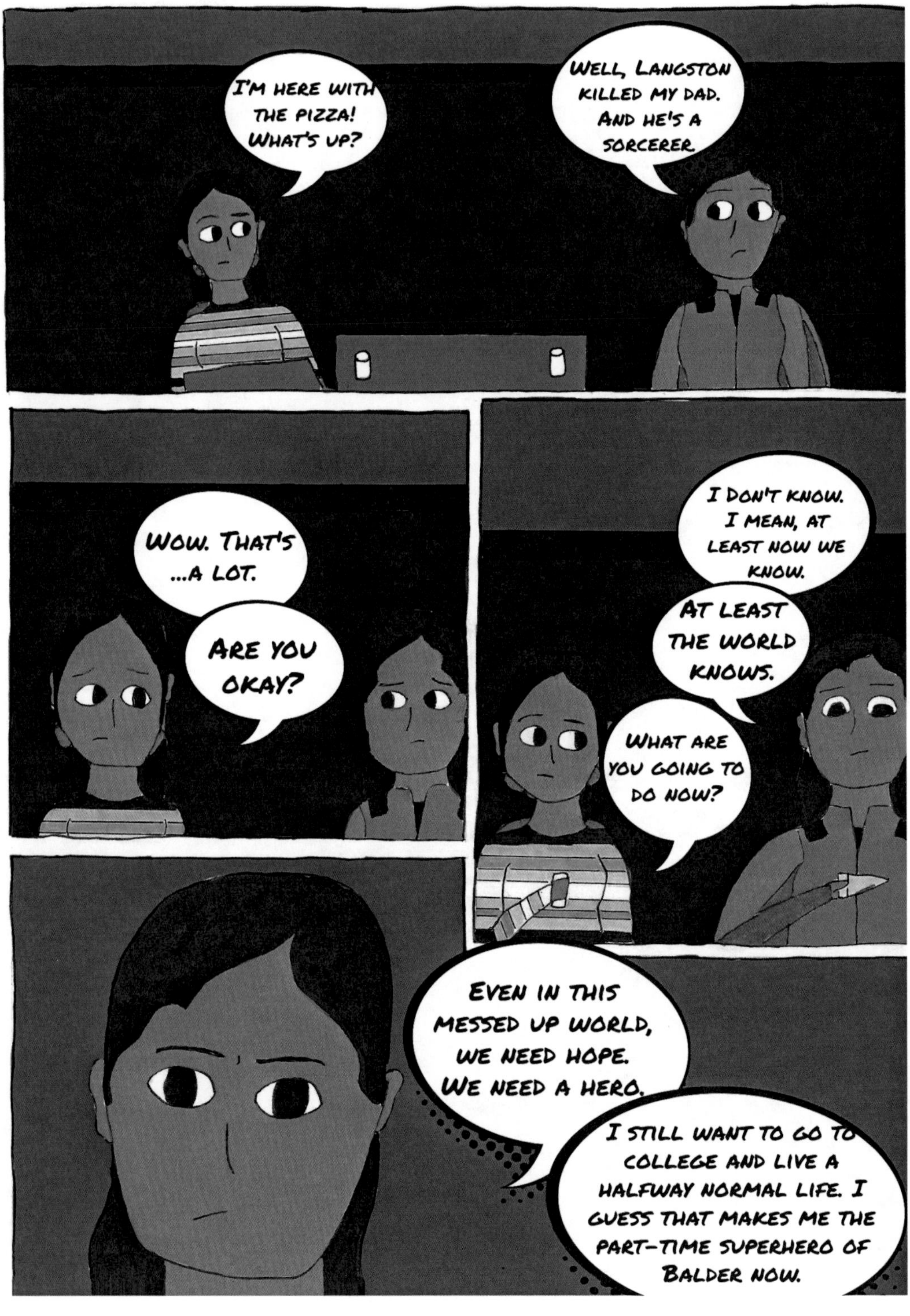
I'M HERE WITH THE PIZZA! WHAT'S UP?
WELL, LANGSTON KILLED MY DAD. AND HE'S A SORCERER.
WOW. THAT'S ...A LOT.
ARE YOU OKAY?
I DON'T KNOW. I MEAN, AT LEAST NOW WE KNOW.
AT LEAST THE WORLD KNOWS.
WHAT ARE YOU GOING TO DO NOW?
EVEN IN THIS MESSED UP WORLD, WE NEED HOPE. WE NEED A HERO.
I STILL WANT TO GO TO COLLEGE AND LIVE A HALFWAY NORMAL LIFE. I GUESS THAT MAKES ME THE PART-TIME SUPERHERO OF BALDER NOW.

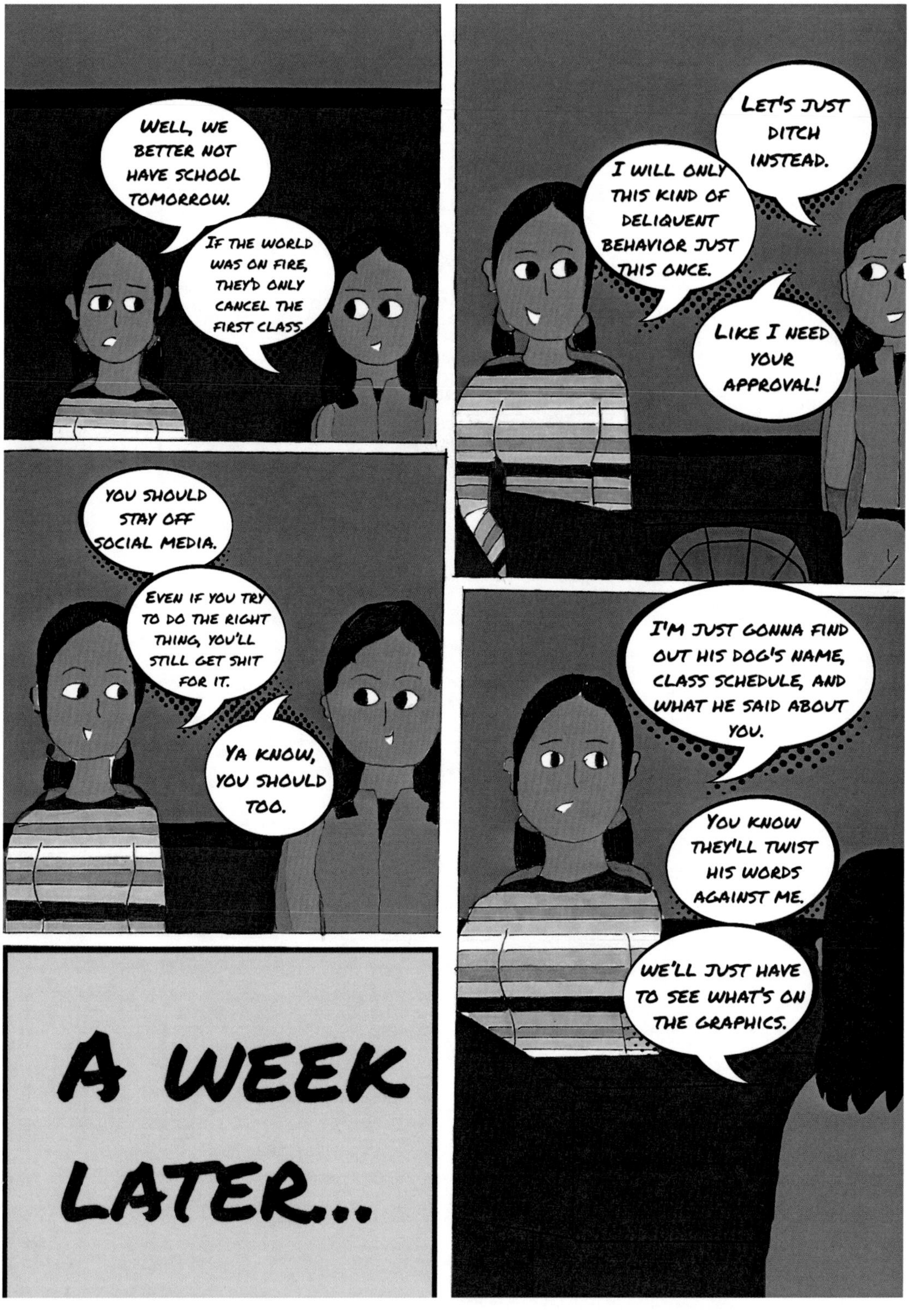
WELL, WE BETTER NOT HAVE SCHOOL TOMORROW.
IF THE WORLD WAS ON FIRE, THEY'D ONLY CANCEL THE FIRST CLASS.
LET'S JUST DITCH INSTEAD.
I WILL ONLY THIS KIND OF DELIQUENT BEHAVIOR JUST THIS ONCE.
LIKE I NEED YOUR APPROVAL!
YOU SHOULD STAY OFF SOCIAL MEDIA.
EVEN IF YOU TRY TO DO THE RIGHT THING, YOU'LL STILL GET SHIT FOR IT.
YA KNOW, YOU SHOULD TOO.
I'M JUST GONNA FIND OUT HIS DOG'S NAME, CLASS SCHEDULE, AND WHAT HE SAID ABOUT YOU.
YOU KNOW THEY'LL TWIST HIS WORDS AGAINST ME.
WE'LL JUST HAVE TO SEE WHAT'S ON THE GRAPHICS.
A WEEK LATER...

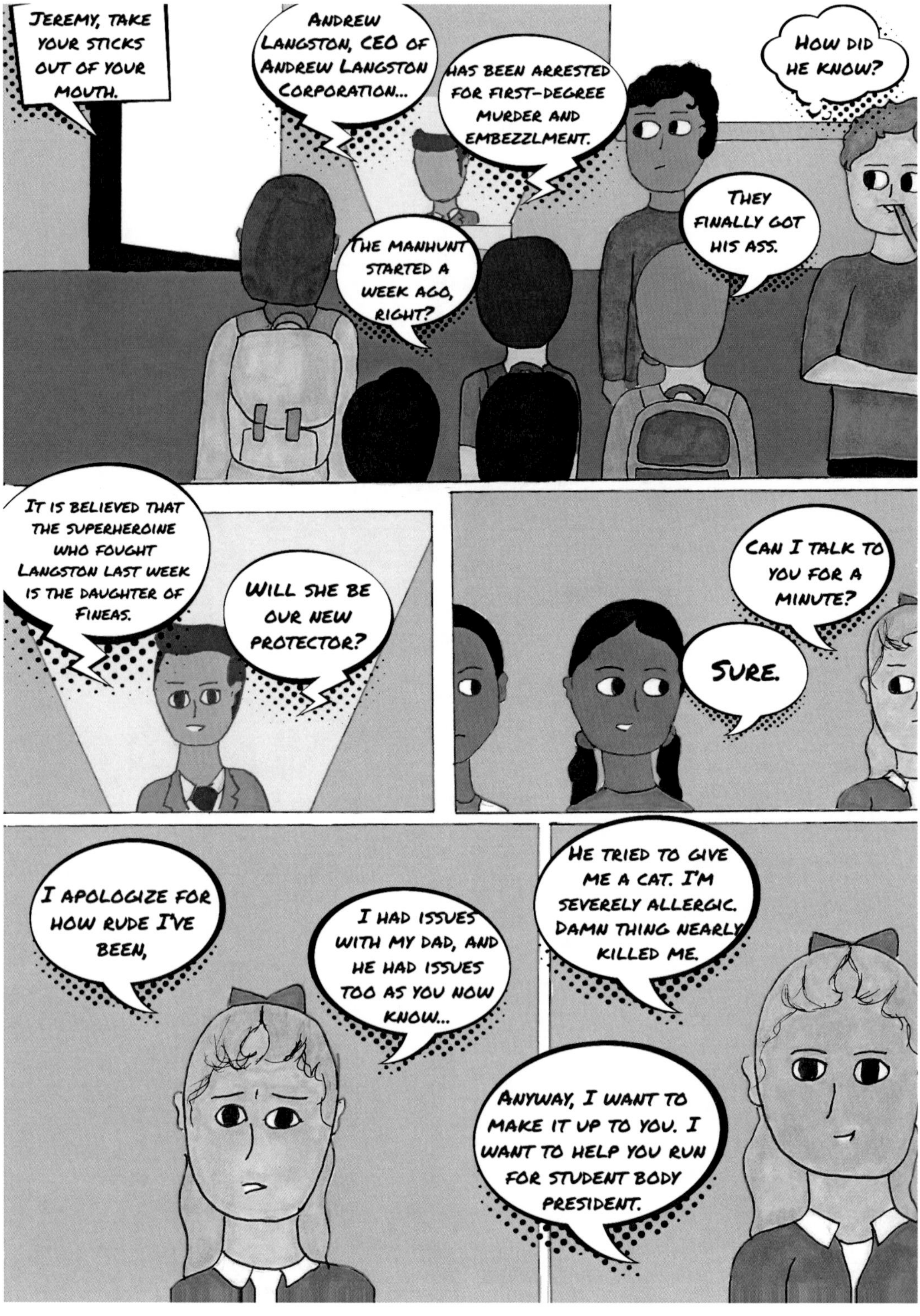

Jeremy, take your sticks out of your mouth.
Andrew Langston, CEO of Andrew Langston Corporation...
has been arrested for first-degree murder and embezzlment.
How did he know?
They finally got his ass.
The manhunt started a week ago, right?
It is believed that the superheroine who fought Langston last week is the daughter of Fineas.
Will she be our new protector?
Can I talk to you for a minute?
Sure.
I apologize for how rude I've been,
I had issues with my dad, and he had issues too as you now know...
He tried to give me a cat. I'm severely allergic. Damn thing nearly killed me.
Anyway, I want to make it up to you. I want to help you run for student body president.

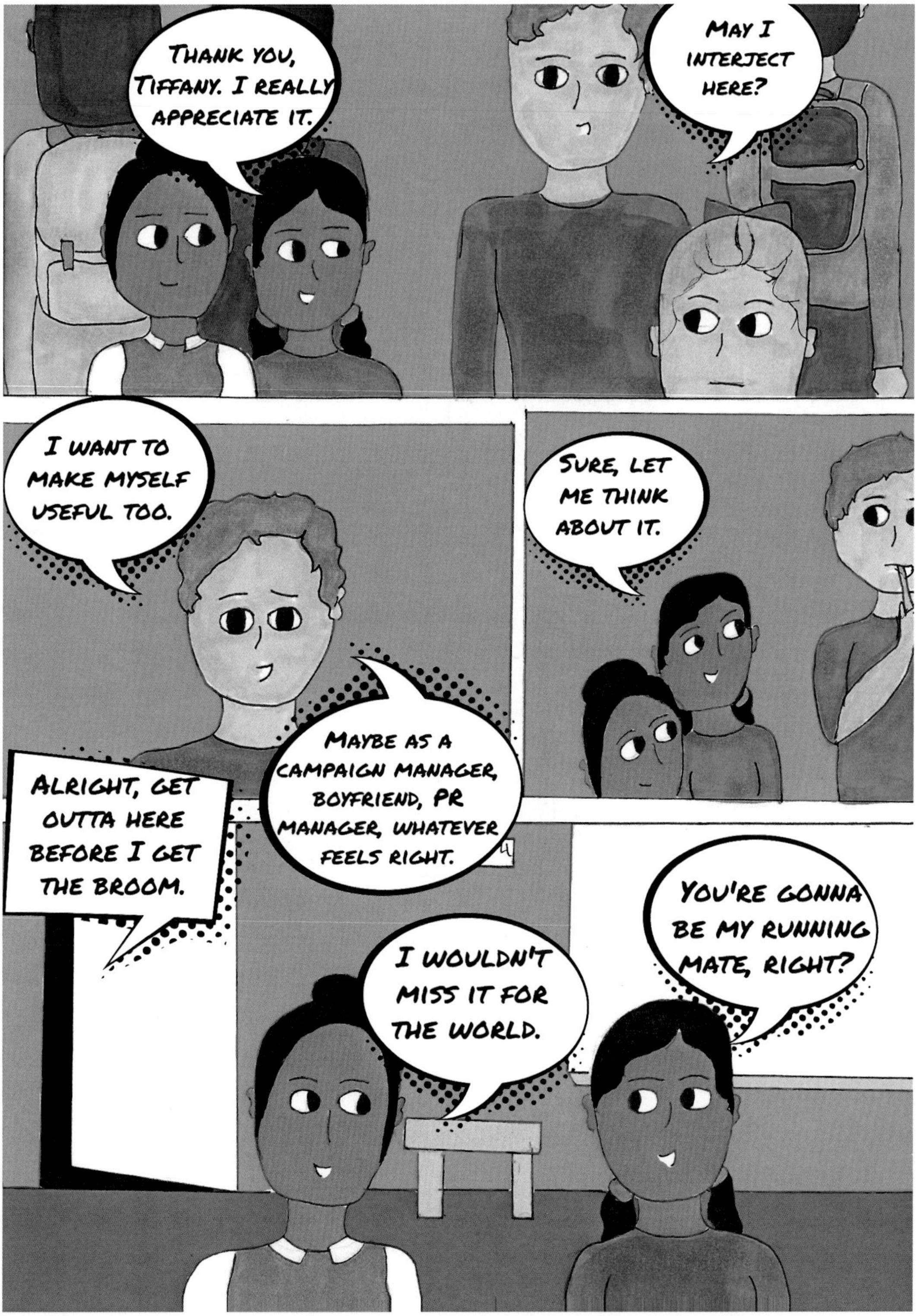
THANK YOU, TIFFANY. I REALLY APPRECIATE IT.
MAY I INTERJECT HERE?
I WANT TO MAKE MYSELF USEFUL TOO.
MAYBE AS A CAMPAIGN MANAGER, BOYFRIEND, PR MANAGER, WHATEVER FEELS RIGHT.
SURE, LET ME THINK ABOUT IT.
ALRIGHT, GET OUTTA HERE BEFORE I GET THE BROOM.
YOU'RE GONNA BE MY RUNNING MATE, RIGHT?
I WOULDN'T MISS IT FOR THE WORLD.

VARIANT COVER BY
ALIE MISKIE

Cover Art by Alie Miskie

About the Author

The author Jessica Johnson was an Ambassador level Girl Scout working on her Gold Award Project. She wrote a comic book called The Rise of Sorceress that features a woman of color superhero named Lucy Davis to bring attention to racial and women's issues. She also wrote it to inspire young women of color and women in general to rise up to the challenges that they face in today's society.

"I wrote The Rise of Sorceress because I wanted to read about a superhero that looked like me. As a comic book lover myself, I noticed that a majority of superheroes are men and are white. I wanted to have a story that minorities could relate to and be inspired from. I also find it empowering to have role models who aren't afraid to vocalize their struggles and successes. Even though Lucy isn't real, the struggles she goes through are. I wanted to shine a light on the struggles to acknowledge them but also to inspire others to make a change in their communities." - Jessica Johnson